Consciousness & Choice

Finding Your Soulmate

Rabbi Yitzchak Ginsburgh

THE TEACHINGS OF KABBALAH SERIES

by Rabbi Yitzchak Ginsburgh

The Hebrew Letters
Channels of Creative Consciousness

The Mystery of Marriage
How to Find True Love and Happiness in Married Life

Awakening the Spark Within
Five Dynamics of Leadership That Can Change the World

Transforming Darkness into Light
Kabbalah and Psychology

Rectifying the State of Israel
A Political Platform based on Kabbalah

Living in Divine Space
Kabbalah and Meditation

Body, Mind, and Soul
Kabbalah on Human Physiology, Disease, and Healing

Consciousness & Choice
Finding Your Soulmate

Consciousness & Choice

Finding Your Soulmate

Rabbi Yitzchak Ginsburgh

Gal Einai Institute
Jerusalem

THE TEACHINGS OF KABBALAH SERIES

CONSCIOUSNESS & CHOICE: FINDING YOUR SOULMATE

RABBI YITZCHAK GINSBURGH
Editors: Yechezkel Anis and Moshe Genuth

Printed in the United States of America and Israel
First Edition

For information:

USA: GAL EINAI
       PO Box 41
       Cedarhurst, NY 11516-9862,
       tel/fax (toll-free): (888) 453-0571

Israel: GAL EINAI
          PO Box 1015
          Kfar Chabad 72915
          tel. (in Israel): 1-700-700-966
          tel. (from abroad): 972-3-9608008

email: inner@inner.org.

Web: www.inner.org

GAL EINAI produces and publishes books, pamphlets, audiocassettes and videocassettes by Rabbi Yitzchak Ginsburgh. To receive a catalog of our products in English and/or Hebrew, please contact us at any of the above addresses, email orders@inner.org or call our orders department in Israel.

ISBN: 965-7146-097

Table of Contents

Preface

Many is the modern physicist who would tell you that without some form of consciousness overlooking reality nothing would exist. Not only does consciousness bring the basic building blocks of our physical universe into existence but it also chooses and directs the paths they take. When it comes to ideas, it is consciousness that guides the course of events necessary for turning them into a reality.

All of this is familiar territory to Judaism and its inner wisdom, Kabbalah. The literal meaning of God's essential Name, *Havayah*, is that He brings all of reality into existence, continuously.[1] But, the great medieval Kabbalist, Rabbi Abraham Abulafia, taught that the four letters of this Name, *Havayah*, stand for the initials of the phrase "He is the single one and knows all."[2] This seemingly paradoxical phrase, declares at one and the same time the singularity of the Creator and His omniscience of all beings. Taken together, the literal and Kabbalistic interpretations inform us that it is the Creator's consciousness itself that not only permeates and knows all that is, but actually brings it into being.

In the language of Jewish philosophy: "He knows all (is conscious of all) by knowing Himself."[3] He does so by means of His consciousness—His creative power and Divine Providence—which in truth is no other than He Himself.[4]

Though every creature possesses a certain degree of consciousness, man was gifted with the highest level of consciousness in creation. Upon creating man, God brought all the animals on earth to Adam to give each a name.[5] A being's proper name in Hebrew is the channel of Divine consciousness by which it is continuously created and sustained.[6] Thus the ability to recognize each animal's name identifies the proximity of Adam's initial consciousness to the Creator's.

Going a step further, the sages relate that once Adam had finished naming the animals God inquired: "And what is My Name?!" Knowing his Creator, Adam answered, "It is fitting to call You *Adonai* [*Lord*], for You are the Master of the universe."[7] This interpretive addendum to what is related in the Torah is an almost obvious allusion to the unfathomable responsibility that human consciousness carries with it.

The ability to exercise our capacity for choice is directly proportional to our success in developing and revealing our consciousness. Every time we approach a crossroad in life, we are faced with decision: do we turn to the "right," or to the "left." In a certain sense, every choice we make is a naming process. We name things generically (not specifically, as did Adam), calling them "good" or "bad," "right" or "wrong." Human consciousness is continuously engaged in making such value judgments. As we shall see, "value" exists on all planes of consciousness, as intellectual value, emotional value, or pragmatic value. By calling something "right," we mean that it is the right thing for us to do, or involve ourselves with, in a given situation. We go on to affirm our decision by saying "yes" or "no."[8]

To say "yes" to something from the depth of one's heart—whether it be to God and His Torah, to one's spouse-to-be, or to a choice of vocation—is to create an existential bond with the object of that choice. The choice to marry is essentially related to Adam's ability to call things by name. Giving names to other creatures was a build-up to the creation of Eve from Adam's own flesh and bones, and Adam calling her "woman" (*ishah*) because she came from his own self called "man" (*ish*). By calling Eve by name, Adam expressed his conscious choice to marry her.

Marriage is not only about choosing a partner for life, but to sow seeds for all future generations.[9] We marry in order to procreate (spiritually and/or physically).[10] In procreating we emulate our Creator because we choose to reflect Him in ourselves. Indeed, the Creator chose to create us out of the desire that we, in our finitude, reflect Him, in His infinity, by being fruitful and multiplying.[11] Thus, the ideal model for studying how consciousness unfolds and creates our reality is that of choosing a soulmate.

ﹻ   ﹻ   ﹻ

Part I of this book examines the steps involved in the unfolding of consciousness/the decision-making process, touching upon the three general types of choice we make in life: spiritual choice, personal choice, and practical choice.

Part II applies the theoretical process to the specific example of how to choose a soulmate. More than any other matrix of choice, finding a soulmate incorporates all three levels of choice: spiritual, personal, and practical.

The in-depth exploration of this example is meant to, by extension, shed light on the other fundamental decisions we make in life: choosing a belief system to mold our character and guide us along the path of life, or choosing a vocation and finding meaning in a career.

ﻼ   ﻼ   ﻼ

Historically, this book is based first and foremost on a series of classes on Jewish jurisprudence given some thirty years ago by Rabbi Ginsburgh to a group of legal professionals, lawyers, and judges in Kfar Chabad. Over a decade later a series of lectures on decision theory was given to a group of professors at the Faculty of Management, Tel-Aviv University, and then the material was taught in greater depth to students of the *Od Yosef Chai* Yeshiva in Shechem.

One of the products of those classes was a terse 30-page article titled *Partzuf Hada'at* which was later published in Rabbi Ginsburgh's Hebrew volume, *Sha'arei Ahava Veratzon*. This article, subtitled "The Decision-Making Process," became the foundation for a graduate-level course in decision theory at Tel Aviv University taught by one of Rabbi Ginsburgh's students, Prof. Gabriel Handler.

Thanks to the resilience of another of Rabbi Ginsburgh's students, Yechezkel Anis, the decision-making process was applied to the process of finding a soulmate. Yechezkel Anis also wrote the first draft of this present volume.

In addition to Yechezkel Anis and Prof. Gabriel Handler, we wish to thank Rabbi Asher and Mrs. Sara Esther Crispe, Mrs. Uriela Sagiv, and Rabbi Moshe Wisnefsky, for their invaluable editorial assistance.

ھ   ھ   ھ

The present volume complements our earlier book *The Mystery of Marriage* that focuses predominantly on life as a married couple, based on the teachings of Kabbalah and Chassidut.

Our hope is to continue to shed light from a traditional Jewish perspective, opening up the wellsprings of the Kabbalistic tradition for the benefit of the entire world.

Editor's Note

We have observed the following conventions in this book:

• Several Names for God are used in the Bible and referred to here. Because of their holiness and spiritual power, it is forbidden to pronounce these Names other than in prayer or when reciting a complete Biblical verse. Therefore, we have deliberately altered the transliteration of these Names, in accordance with the time-honored practice of how observant Jews pronounce them in non-liturgical contexts.

The unique, four-letter Name of God is known generally as the Tetragrammaton and is referred to in Jewish writings (and in this book, as well) as "the Name *Havayah*." We are forbidden to pronounce this Name altogether, and indeed, its correct pronunciation is not known nowadays; in liturgical contexts, the Name *Adni* is pronounced in its place. Due to its special sanctity, it has been intentionally abbreviated as הוי' in verses quoted in Hebrew. When two different names of God appear in the same verse, we have spelled it with large and small capitals ("GOD") in order to distinguish it (e.g., p. 37).

• The term "Bible" (*Tanach*) comprises the Torah (the Five Books of Moses); the Prophets (consisting of eight books: Joshua, Judges, Samuel, Kings, Isaiah, Jeremiah, Ezekiel, and the Twelve Prophets); and the Writings (consisting of eleven books: Psalms, Proverbs, Job, Ruth, the

Song of Songs, Ecclesiastes, Lamentations, Esther, Daniel, Ezra-Nehemiah, and Chronicles).

• The term "Torah" must be understood according to the context: in its narrowest sense, it refers to the Five Books of Moses, but more generally, it can refer to the entirety of God's written and orally transmitted teachings to Israel and all of humanity.

• The term "Kabbalah" is sometimes used in its specific sense, to refer to the classic texts of the ancient Jewish mystical tradition, and sometimes in its more general sense, to refer to the whole of the inner dimension of the Torah, including the teachings of Chassidut. Indeed, Chassidut is referred to in Chassidic texts as "the Kabbalah of the Ba'al Shem Tov,"[12] inasmuch as its revelation of the innermost core of faith and wisdom lies at the base of all the classic texts of Kabbalah.

• Unlike previous volumes, in the interest of retaining the readability of the text and its flow, we have kept to a minimum the use of transliteration in the text, except for the first time that a well-known concept in Kabbalah or Chassidut appears. This includes the transliteration of the Hebrew words for the *sefirot*. It is left to the reader to use the various explanations and usages of the different terms in order to construct the meaning that each carries. For example on p. 1 the *sefirah* of *da'at* is explained to mean either "knowledge" or "consciousness." Later in the text we either refer to it as the "*sefirah* of knowledge" (see pp. 22, 32, 69, 113, 127) or just as "consciousness." However, not every mention of consciousness necessarily implies the "*sefirah* of *da'at.*" Nonetheless, in all cases some affinity to *da'at* can be assumed.

In hope of making the text more readable, we have not placed the names of the *sefirot* and other Kabbalistic and Chassidic terminology in quotes, as was done in previous volumes.

• We have formatted the text differently from *The Mystery of Marriage* (this book's companion volume). All footnotes appear at the end of the book, arranged by chapter and page number for easy reference. Citations and material that directly relate to the flow of the text were included in the endnotes, while supplementary essays at the end of the text contain material for the more advanced reader. Also, a glossary at the end of the book defines most of the Hebrew and Kabbalistic terms, and a bibliography is included as reference. Several separate indexes have been included as well.

• Finally, Hebrew words are written out in *ktiv chaser*, as they would be spelled in the Bible and, where appropriate, appear with vowel signs for easier reading. When a Hebrew word appears in a bold type-face, this denotes the word's or words' numerical (*gematria*) value. A table of the Hebrew letters' values appears in the glossary under the entry for *gematria.*

ક્ર   ક્ર   ક્ર

The following story is told of the great *tzadik*, Reb Hirsch Leib Aliker, a disciple of the Maggid of Mezheritch:

As a child, Reb Hirsch was raised by his grandparents. Once he overheard his grandparents discussing the fact that he was ready for marriage, but unfortunately was short—something that would impair his chances of finding a good *shidduch* (marriage-proposal).

Troubled by what he had heard, Reb Hirsch turned to God that night before going to sleep and said: "Master of the Universe, You can certainly make me taller when I get up tomorrow morning. You need not fear that it would appear like a miracle; people won't even notice what transpired overnight."

When he awoke the next morning, he was indeed taller and soon became engaged and was given a precious gift by his father-in-law. However, he lost the gift and was greatly embarrassed to face his father-in-law.

He stood and said: "Master of the Universe, in Your eyes all places are as one, wherever the gift is, You can bring it here. People will simply assume that here is where I lost it." And, before finishing his words, the gift appeared.

The Sadigora Rebbe, Reb Avraham Yaakov, said that telling this story of the *tzadik* Reb Hirsch Aliker, is itself a *segulah* (good) for finding whatever one has lost.

There is no doubt that the trials and tribulations associated with finding a spouse are some of the most difficult ones that Jewish men and women face today. This is oftentimes especially true for those who have decided to become *ba'alei teshuvah* and to embrace the Torah's way of life in body and spirit at a more mature age. Though numerous "technical" solutions are offered (friends "setting-up" dates, "speed-dating," etc.) in the end, responsibility lies only in the hands of that individual who wishes to build his or her home.

Finding a spouse is akin to finding one's own self; in the words of the *tzadik* quoted above: "…in the very spot where something is lost there it is found." Finding one's self is dependent on the development of consciousness—the two are intertwined and go hand-in-hand. For we who believe in Divine Providence and in God's ultimate goodness, there is always the comfort that we each possess a *beshert*—a pre-destined soulmate. But, unlike the love-at-first-sight vision most often sold today, Divinely ordained love demands that we reveal our own Divine essence in order to recognize the hidden bond with our soulmate. Surprisingly, there is nothing less obvious, at first sight, than the eternal relationship of two people destined to be with one another throughout this lifetime and in the World-to-Come.

It is no secret that our psychological and spiritual state affects the way we see the world. Similarly, the ability to "find" our soulmate, to recognize him or her for who they are to us (and likewise, to be "found," to be recognized for who we are), is an active one. It serves as a measure of our own essential connection and relationship with our Creator, and shapes, and even alters, the reality we live in. In the words of the sages (*Megillah* 6b): "if one says 'I have toiled but have not found'—do not believe him," i.e., do not believe that he has toiled sufficiently. It follows therefore, that if someone has indeed toiled (to the best of his ability), then something has changed in his reality, and "finding" is immanent.

Because finding a soulmate depends on developing our consciousness and finding out who we are, things can (and do) change overnight, like in the story told above. The way other people perceive us (even physically) is dependent on how we relate to the Divine, on how well we attune our consciousness to the Divine life-force that permeates everything that we are and that makes up our world. All in all, the conscious stance that we adopt when standing as Jews before our Creator, plays the central role in getting married.

Other guides to finding a soulmate may seem more "down to earth" and better at describing, and perhaps even advising, the reader as to specific hands-on events and feelings that people encounter while dating and making a decision about marriage. This book, however, does not intend to provide concrete advice about who, how or when to date. Rather, it is about self-transformation, and how it affects our conscious perception of those individuals we find ourselves with when searching for our *beshert*.

Similar to almost all of Rabbi Ginsburgh's work, the writing in this volume is predominantly contemplative in its nature. As such, it may seem overly theoretical. However, Jewish tradition in general and Kabbalah and Chassidut in particular, maintain that real change and growth start with contemplation. It is the mind that ultimately informs the heart about reality, and governs and directs our thought, speech, and actions. More importantly, it is through contemplation that consciousness unfolds and develops quickest. As such, mindful reading and rereading of this text during a relationship are sure to facilitate the "creation" of a mature and responsible yet at the same time "living and breathing" approach to the dating process, and to the great challenge that it brings: finding your soulmate.

Like all the teachings we have merited to hear over the years from Rabbi Ginsburgh, the contents of this book are born out of deep contemplation of the Torah's secrets, and a profound trust that the Torah is indeed the ultimate source of all our wisdom and understanding, as Jews. It is offered with the sincere faith taught by the Ba'al Shem Tov: that everything we do in life—including searching for and finding our soulmate—gives us a chance to come closer to the Infinite Light of God.

Moshe Genuth
Jerusalem
15 *Av*, 5764

Introduction

The Seat of Consciousness

In the terminology of Kabbalah, our ability to make decisions is a function of the spiritual power, the *sefirah,* of knowledge (*da'at*), or as it can also be translated, consciousness.[1] It is one in the series of Divine powers or channels of Divine energy known as the ten *sefirot* (in the plural, *sefirah* in the singular) through which God creates reality, as we know it. The *sefirot* constitute the most basic taxonomy of Kabbalah and Chassidut, and form the basic paradigm by which we can analyze all worldly phenomena—most importantly those pertaining to the human psyche.

The *sefirah* of knowledge expresses itself in our psyche as a force of unification (*yichud*).[2] It functions like a multi-level bridge spanning the gap between precognition (super-consciousness, as will be explained) and intellect (*muskal*), between intellect and emotions (*murgash*), and between emotion and behavior (*mutba*). The inner balance and energy-flow between the individual faculties of each of these realms of the psyche is a function of knowledge as well. By bringing into alliance all the powers of the soul, it makes it possible for the soul to interact in this world.

In its role as a unifying force, the *sefirah* of knowledge is the soul's primary arbiter of "choice," as expressed in God's words to Israel, "Only you have I known [*yada'ati,* from knowledge] from all the families of the earth,"[3] meaning

1

"Only you have I chosen...."[4] A proper choice ensues when our consciousness is galvanized so that it helps us express the ideals and goals of our intellect.[5]

Kabbalah speaks of many levels of knowledge. As consciousness, knowledge is present within each of the conscious attributes of the soul (as well as between them, to connect them, as noted). In particular, the unifying force of knowledge operates simultaneously on two planes of consciousness, one concealed (higher) and one revealed (lower):[6]

First, on the concealed plane, located between the two primary faculties of the intellect, wisdom (*chochmah*) and understanding (*binah*),[7] the *sefirah* of knowledge serves to sustain an ongoing collaboration between them, thus producing a state referred to as higher consciousness (*da'at elyon*).[8] This state of consciousness represents the most refined state of enlightenment attainable, making it possible for the intellect to assert itself as virtually independent of the emotions and instincts through which it is normally filtered.[9] In so doing, it allows the soul to penetrate the illusions to which our sensual experience of reality gives rise, and to come to know the pure truth of reality's Divine origin.[10]

Secondly, on the revealed plane, the *sefirah* of knowledge operates as the mediator between the intellect (mind) and the emotions (heart). Here, knowledge acts as a force of integration, promoting a harmony between our psyche and our surroundings.[11] This form of unification is referred to as lower consciousness (*da'at tachton*).[12] We experience this aspect of knowledge as the subjective consciousness of our seemingly independent "self" in its interactions with the outside world. When functioning optimally, this aspect of our consciousness allows for balanced and responsible interactions with others—interactions that reflect the influence of our intellect on the lower forces of emotion and instinct.

In Proverbs, King Solomon, the wisest of men, says, "Without knowledge the soul is not good."[13] The unifying power of knowledge is here identified with "good" (*tov*).[14] Both levels of consciousness are inherently good. The goodness of higher consciousness is the goodness of the mind, while that of lower consciousness is the goodness of the heart. Of the goodness of the mind it is said, "Teach me good reason and knowledge."[15] Of the goodness of the heart it is said that God desires that we serve Him "with joy and a good heart."[16] Of course, in order to serve God we must first know Him by nurturing our consciousness of the Divine.[17]

When speaking of a good person, we generally mean a person with a good heart. Accordingly, Kabbalah depicts the *sefirah* of knowledge as poised midway between those *sefirot* linked with the mind and those linked with the heart.[18] As such, knowledge is metaphorically described as the key of the mind that opens the chambers of the heart[19] and fills them with goodness, a faculty hinted to in the verse: "Through knowledge chambers are filled with all precious and pleasant riches."[20] As we shall explain, this "key" metaphor alludes to the fact that knowledge has the power to unlock the figurative "doors" of our heart, as the decision process unfolds to include the emotive powers (the lower *sefirot*) related to the heart.

Consciousness As a Persona (*Partzuf*)

One of the most important concepts in Kabbalah is that of the persona or *partzuf*, and serves to place distinct entities in a contextual framework.[21] Without the concept of the *partzuf*, a *sefirah* stands as a distinct force precluding any analysis as to its internal structure and its relationship to other *sefirot*/forces. With the *partzuf* we can both view each sefirah as part of a structural model allowing us to analyze its relations and interactions with the other *sefirot*; and we are able to analyze the *sefirah* itself as a higher-level structure that contains internal functionality and structure. In Kabbalistic terminology the internal structure of a *sefirah* is holographic, in the sense that it echoes the general structure of the 10 *sefirot*.

This volume treats the *sefirah* of knowledge, or the phenomenon of our consciousness, as a *partzuf*. Doing so reveals the *sefirah* of knowledge comprises the following structure:

keter shebe'da'at
crown of knowledge

binah shebe'da'at
understanding of knowledge

chochmah shebe'da'at
wisdom of knowledge

da'at shebe'da'at
knowledge of knowledge

gevurah shebe'da'at
strength of knowledge

chesed shebe'da'at
loving-kindness of knowledge

tiferet shebe'da'at
beauty of knowledge

hod shebe'da'at
thanksgiving of knowledge

netzach shebe'da'at
victory of knowledge

yesod shebe'da'at
foundation of knowledge

malchut shebe'da'at
kingdom of knowledge

The *partzuf* of knowledge is seen here to be composed of eleven interrelated *sefirot*.[22]

Though every *sefirah* can be analyzed as a complete *partzuf*, the *partzuf* of knowledge stands unique in that there exists a well-utilised and well-known Hebrew idiom that specifically corresponds to (and describes) each of its eleven *sefirot*. This linguistic phenomenon reflects the fact that knowledge is indeed the most all-inclusive of the *sefirot*, most naturally lending itself to the construction of a complete *partzuf*. These eleven idioms when seen to evolve logically one from the other, serve as the ideal model to represent the decision-making process, the soul's unfolding of consciousness.

The best way then to understand how consciousness impacts our decision-making, is to chart the process by which all of the *sefirot* relate in the context of the *partzuf* of knowledge. Thus, the final step in this introduction will be to correspond each of the *sefirot* of the *partzuf* of knowledge with a specific stage in the process by which consciousness unfolds. They do so in three stages:

- First, consciousness seeks out its Divine roots in order to draw inspiration for the ongoing dialogue between the inner self and outer reality;

- Next, it confronts and processes reality (this is where it considers and selects a particular course of action);

- Finally, consciousness takes theoretical choice, tests it, modifies it, and ultimately transforms it into a clear decision.

The stages of this process are linked with the various descriptive idioms of knowledge, the inter-inclusion of all the *sefirot* within knowledge, as follows:

crown of knowledge
(super-consciousness)
deepening

understanding of knowledge   wisdom of knowledge
stability   expansion

knowledge of knowledge
attachment

strength of knowledge   loving-kindness of knowledge
objectivity   affinity

beauty of knowledge
appraisal

thanksgiving of knowledge   victory of knowledge
concurrence   resolve

foundation of knowledge
decision

kingdom of knowledge
expression

For the sake of clarity and completeness we have written out the process of the unfolding of consciousness in flowchart format, including the Hebrew idioms that are the original terms marking the flow from level to level:

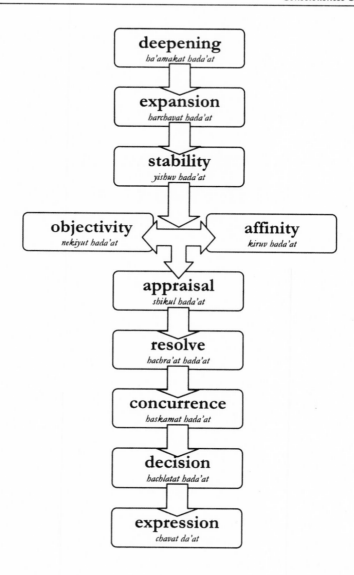

PART I

Consciousness
and Decision-Making

1

Super-Consciousness

The Roots of Consciousness

The first of the ten *sefirot* described in Kabbalah, the crown (*keter*), is reflected in the soul by the realm we call super-consciousness. The term super-consciousness aptly conveys the transcendent character of this realm hovering above, yet directly influencing consciousness.

In the super-conscious realm of the crown, the pristine, pre-verbal self resides in mute autonomy, detached from the world around it but connected to its Divine source.

Out of this seemingly impenetrable core of self-isolation evolves consciousness, which recognizes the meaningful and independent existence of others with whom it aspires to form attachments. Emanating from within the depths of the crown at the point where it touches God's Infinite Light and His will to create, a signal commands the super-conscious realm to relinquish its exclusive state of aloneness for the sake of togetherness.

The emergence of consciousness out of self-isolation is a process that recurs at various stages of life, bringing ever-increasing degrees of responsibility. Physical birth precipitates the first emergence of consciousness, albeit deficient and undeveloped.[1] The vulnerability of this nascent consciousness lasts until we reach the age of physical, intellectual, and moral maturity that allows a proper assumption of responsibility in our relations with God and people. Interestingly, the Hebrew word for responsibility (*achrayut*), is related at its root to the word for other (*acher*), hinting at the sensitivity to others that must inform all mature and responsible action.[2]

The states of super-consciousness (being-in-oneself) and consciousness (being-in-the-world) appear to be both separate *and* interdependent. How could the self be propelled out of its super-conscious isolation if the seed of consciousness did not exist in super-consciousness?[3] Conversely, from where would the mature consciousness get its ability to identify with and connect to the outside world if it did not retain some impression of super-consciousness, imbuing it with the belief that all of creation derives from the same Divine source?

If there is any appearance of a conflict between super-consciousness and consciousness, it stems from the different way in which each processes reality. The perfect image of creation rests hidden within super-consciousness, waiting to find reflection in the outer world through the vehicle of "rectified" consciousness—that is, a consciousness that has come full circle and rediscovered the Divine face of creation. But in order for that to happen, consciousness must first establish dominance within the soul. This means that the vision of super-consciousness must remain veiled, so that it may inspire without shattering our hold on the here-and-now.

When consciousness completes its work of rectification in this world—a process known in Kabbalah as *tikun*—we will become able to perceive the ideal form behind what we call reality. At that time, we will behold the vision of super-consciousness: the oneness and perfection of the entirety of creation. In the meantime, our ability to balance the opposing drives of super-consciousness and consciousness—the temptation to recede into the sweet oblivion of the womb of Eden and the need to continue the hard work of our conscious mission—enables our essential self to remain in communion with its Divine source while maintaining relationships with others, separate from that self.[4]

Deepening of Consciousness

The first step in achieving a meaningful bond with outer reality involves acknowledging the existential gulf that separates the essential self from its surroundings. Only then can we recognize the source of consciousness in super-consciousness and begin to understand the mystery and miracle at work here.

The process whereby consciousness explores its own origins in super-consciousness, and in so doing enhances its ability to connect thereafter to outer reality, is referred to as the deepening of consciousness (*ha'amakat hada'at*). Deepening corresponds to the *sefirah* of the crown within the *partzuf* of knowledge,[5] the point in the soul where super-consciousness and consciousness touch.

The deepening of consciousness—that is, reaching the point where consciousness interacts with super-consciousness—requires selflessness.[6] Selflessness, or absence of ego, gives us the power to transcend the distorted image of the self that is the product of conscious experience in order that our true self—that is, the soul—can come to the fore. In the depth of consciousness, we can force our conscious self to "shut its eyes"[7] as it were, and commune with our soul-essence. There, at the interface between the soul and its Divine source, exists a window on eternity from where we can see with the "eyes of the soul"[8] and scan the absolute unity of all creation in a single glance.

If we are willing to momentarily suspend the ties that bind us to the world of thought, we can reach this inner space where lies the seed of all future knowledge. The plane of super-consciousness represents both the undifferentiated seed from which consciousness evolves, as well as the supreme end to which it aspires—knowledge of the "unknowable."

But if we are bound too closely to the realm of immediate experience, a free fall into the domain of super-consciousness can represent a terrible threat. The promise of discovering our soul-root in the Divine abstraction that underlies creation may then seem like an invitation to chaos, an endless slide into a maelstrom from which we might never emerge.[9] To the devotees of concrete reality, the infinite expanse of super-consciousness is a terrifying, uncharted wilderness—a white-light convergence of possibilities and paths—where they are likely to feel hopelessly stranded, unable to map a course back to knowledge and identity.[10]

Yet deepening represents more than a retreat from what is known and familiar; it represents the opportunity to advance conscious knowledge as well. Knowledge of the world requires more than the gathering of data from our field of observation. It requires a continuous connection between the super-conscious image of reality imprinted on our soul and the conscious image of reality that comes from lived experience. This is why knowledge is often advanced by startling and inscrutable spurts of intuition.

Excessive preoccupation with external experience blocks access to the well of inspiration that comes from super-consciousness. By deepening our consciousness, we can tap this hidden reservoir and learn to live, as *chassidim* say, *in velt, oys velt,* "in the world and outside the world," simultaneously. When we do, we realize that there is no innate conflict between being-in-oneself and being-in-the-world—the former, in fact, is a springboard to the latter.

Since every soul originates in infinite, Divine reality, its root contains the touchstone of all knowledge and experience. Stripping ourselves of ego lays bare our essential self and allows us to rediscover our fundamental connection with all of creation. Once we reach into the depth of consciousness and touch its source, we can reemerge with a confidence in the ability of our conscious self to recognize instantly those elements of experience that reflect that connection most clearly. Then, subsequent interaction with those elements will prove infinitely more productive and fulfilling.

The Three Strata of Super-Consciousness

Within super-consciousness, there are three strata of inner experience that act as a bridge with consciousness: faith (*emunah*); pleasure (*ta'anug*); and will (*ratzon*). These three correspond in Kabbalah to the three heads of the crown (*tlat reishin de'keter*).

super-consciousness
faith
pleasure
will
consciousness

The two lower strata of pleasure and will are the source of the apparent conflict between being-in-oneself and being-in-the-world.[11] This is because pleasure—which refers to the insular delight of the soul as it revels in its bond with God's Infinite Light—impels us to identify with the abstract essence of reality, which is beyond the grasp of routine awareness. At the same time, will—where the desire for physical experience and the exercise of free-will is born—impels us to identify with the created finite realm.

In mirroring God's Infinite Light, transcendent pleasure experiences the essence of the seven forms of creative energy,[12] which are responsible for all that God fashioned during the seven days of creation. These seven forms of creative energy assert themselves at every level of creation; for instance, on the psychological level, these forces manifest themselves as love, awe, compassion, confidence, sincerity, devotion, and humility.[13] For pleasure to experience the essence of these energies, as they exist in God's Infinite Light before the beginning of the creative process, demands that it have absolute autonomy from the limitations of consciousness, thus granting us, as finite beings, the ability to touch our source in the infinite.

But, if we are truly to relate to these energies, we must forsake the paradise of abstraction represented by pleasure and enter the domain of super-conscious will and of physical experience. It is this will that, at its most elementary level, generates and sustains consciousness itself.

In truth, hidden deep within pleasure lies a desire to share what the soul finds in bonding with God's creative design. The process that makes this sharing possible is called enclothement (*hitlabshut*), whereby the seven forms of creative energy descend into, and become enclothed by will— the will to become manifest in external reality—in the same way that the soul descends into, and is enclothed by, the body.[14] The product of this fusion is the longing of the soul for the pleasures of true knowledge and genuine relationship.[15]

Once the amorphous nirvana of pleasure is tempered by the actualizing force of will, it gains the ability to derive infinite pleasure from physical life and conscious experience. Simultaneously, will gains the inspiration it needs to steer consciousness into productive avenues of expression. Without the inspiration of pleasure, will is only a raw force, without reason or direction. But, combined with pleasure, will becomes the active agent of God's purpose, completing the work of creation that He began.[16]

The component of super-consciousness that forces the two conflicting vectors of pleasure and will into resolution is the hidden faith of the soul in the unity of all being. Faith, which is rooted in the highest recesses of super-consciousness, inspires both pleasure and will to share in each other's identity, a holographic process referred to in Kabbalah as inter-inclusion, which enables the unification of all the elements of creation so that each is included within the other.[17]

Only when we simultaneously adhere to both pleasure and will, can meaningful consciousness emerge. If we prevent will from embracing outer experience we preclude consciousness altogether, while denying pleasure can result in an impoverished consciousness, one estranged from its source in God.

The very existence of a super-conscious will, constantly propelling the self into dialogue with its surroundings, serves as insurance against the danger of losing oneself in the boundless abstraction of pleasure. Hence we need not fear it. And, once we overcome the fear of the prospect of retreating into the realm of solitary super-consciousness, we can begin to appreciate this realm as the base from which to launch our interactions with the world.

We can re-enter the conscious plane armed with experience derived from the super-conscious encounter with self. Applying this experience to physical reality enables us to live with an awareness of a greater unity binding our individual soul to the universe at large.

Thus, faith, pleasure, and will are the primal forces of the super-consciousness that inspire our choices and decisions. In particular, each of the three heads of the crown serves as an origin to one of life's three realms of pursuit (which we shall return to in our analysis of the decision-making process):

Faith is the origin of our pursuit of the virtuous (*tov*, literally, "good").[18] This is the sphere that ultimately inspires our choice of religion or a belief system, as such choices reflect the desire for absolute virtue in the form of the essential good. It also inspires our choice of a marital partner when that choice is based on characteristics of lineage or personal qualities.

Pleasure is the origin of our pursuit of that which is pleasurable (*arev*). This sphere inspires our choice of a spiritual guide, usually picked for the "sweetness" of his light. (The word *arev* also means "guarantor," implying that such a mentor is the guarantor of our soul.) It also inspires our choice of a marital partner when that choice is based on appearance and physical attraction.

Will is the origin of our pursuit of the pragmatic and the profitable (*mo'il*). This is the sphere that inspires our choice of vocation, shaped by the practical considerations of what we do best and what we are most likely to succeed in and benefit from. It also inspires our choice of a marital partner when that choice is based on financial considerations or family connections.[19]

2

Wisdom and Understanding

Expansion of Consciousness

Passing from super-consciousness into mature consciousness requires faith in the implicit oneness of inner and outer reality—that is, spiritual and physical reality. Were the super-conscious and conscious realms truly independent, our awareness of reality would lack depth. Without collaboration between them, consciousness standing alone would prove to be painfully deficient.

Indeed, impairment in the relationship between the super-conscious and conscious realms results in an impoverished consciousness. However, a proper relationship between them engenders an expansion of consciousness (*harchavat hada'at*), whereby we emerge from super-consciousness with a wide-angle lens on reality, ready to discover in the outer world a oneness that accords with our inner vision.

An expansion of consciousness results from the positive contraction of the super-conscious self. The paradigm for this process can be found in the Kabbalistic doctrine of contraction (*tzimtzum*), used to explain the process whereby God caused His Infinite Light (*Or Ain Sof*) to contract or withdraw in order to make room for an evolving, finite creation. This act of Divine altruism is what inspires a contraction of our own super-conscious self so that the expansion of consciousness can take place.

The contraction of super-consciousness enables the transition from self-absorption to outer-relationship. At the same time, the muted voice of super-consciousness whispers in the background, a constant reminder of the Divine unity underlying creation. This voice of super-consciousness is the source of all wisdom. The extent to which our consciousness can hear it is dependent upon another manifestation of contraction in the soul—selflessness or absence of ego.

According to Chassidic thought, selflessness (*bitul*) is associated with the *sefirah* of wisdom. Selflessness allows the aperture of wisdom within the soul to widen so that the wisdom of God can penetrate consciousness. It is the awe of God that impels the self to nullify its ego and thus invite in wisdom, as the Book of Psalms states: "The awe of God is the beginning of wisdom."[1]

Selflessness is what allows our intellect to contact its source in super-consciousness, sparking the sudden illumination known as intuitive insight. It is important to note that, in the general scheme of the *sefirot*, the *sefirah* of wisdom precedes the *sefirah* of knowledge and therefore is not considered to be synonymous with consciousness itself. Rather, wisdom is the channel that aligns consciousness with super-consciousness; thus, it allows the transition from the "nothing-ness" of the super-conscious experience of inner reality to the "something-ness" of the conscious experience of outer reality.

The internal wisdom of consciousness, which we have identified with the expansion of consciousness, is what keeps the window of consciousness open as wide as possible. Through the force of selflessness, wisdom shifts the self from the center of consciousness, so that God's Infinite Light can penetrate the soul without interference and inspire genuine knowledge. It is this influx of light that expands consciousness.

As the channel connecting consciousness to super-consciousness, the wisdom of consciousness (the *chochmah sheba'da'at*, experienced as expansion of consciousness) ensures that the Divine radiance of super-consciousness—tapped through the deepening of consciousness—can find its way into creation.

Embracing Diversity

The depth achieved in the deepening of consciousness is directly proportional to the breadth achieved through its expansion.[2] Consciousness evolves not by breaking with super-consciousness but by sinking its roots deeply into that core of selfhood and then branching outward. Like a tree, the deeper the roots, the broader the canopy.[3]

Implicit in its expansion is consciousness' capacity to tolerate diversity—a necessity when contending with the multiple stimuli of normal experience. This capacity is also an essential qualification of leadership, where it manifests itself as the ability to accommodate diversity within the leader's sphere of influence.[4]

This is why, when Moses appealed to God to appoint his successor who would lead the Jewish people into the Land of Israel, he addressed his prayer to the "God of the spirits of all flesh,"[5] particularly emphasizing that God understands the "spirit" or mindset of every individual. In his commentary on the Torah, Rashi writes that Moses in effect said to God, "Master of the Universe, the thought of every individual is known to You, no two being alike. Appoint over them a leader who will tolerate each according to his thinking."

God, in His response to Moses, implicitly confirmed this caveat:[6]

> Take unto you Joshua, the son of Nun, a man in whom the spirit rests, and lay your hand upon him.

The expression "in whom the spirit rests" (רוּחַ בּוֹ) contains the same letters, in the same order, as the word for breadth/expansion (רוֹחַב). Joshua, by virtue of being a "man in whom rests the spirit," embodied the expanded consciousness needed to lead Israel into the Promised Land.[7]

When God first revealed Himself to Moses at the burning bush, He appointed him to redeem the Jewish People from the Egyptian exile and bring them "to a good and wide (רְחָבָה as in expansion or broadening) land, to a land flowing with milk and honey."[8] These two principal appellations of the Land of Israel "good" and "wide" refer, on the spiritual plane, to the unique states of rectified consciousness that the Jewish soul is able to attain in its homeland: "good," in general,[9] and "wide" implying the expansion of consciousness, in particular.

According to tradition, Joshua, who fulfilled the Divine mission entrusted upon Moses to bring the Jewish People into the Land of Israel, married a local convert to Judaism, Rachav (רָחָב), whose name means "wide," clearly alluding to the expansion of consciousness.[10]

The tolerance that is a hallmark of expanded consciousness represents more than a simple accommodation of differences; it implies the embracing of creation's multiplicity before the mind has a chance to impose its own hierarchies. In human relations, this quality achieves its ideal expression in the love of Israel (*ahavat yisrael*) that mandates that every Jew unconditionally embrace every other Jew as an equal member of the Congregation of Israel.

The above approach is not meant to promote the kind of moral neutrality found in most pluralistic systems, which seek to legitimize all differences. Instead, the tolerance of an expanding consciousness suggests that the legitimacy of all individuals is rooted in their shared status as children of one God. It is this shared responsibility for the Divine character of creation that obligates us to be concerned with each other's moral choices, always believing that every soul is essentially perfect, though subject to the distortions of an imperfect human will.

Indeed, this belief requires us to look for the hidden motivation of the soul underlying any deviant action or belief. The peculiarities of human character possess profound spiritual roots that, when improperly cultivated, can lead to misguided behavior. Our first and foremost responsibility lies in affirming the soul that is seeking fulfillment through the misguided behavior; only then should we address the behavior itself.

It is this acknowledgment of our common Divine source that inspires true tolerance that must be accompanied by patience. Tolerance implies the willingness to suffer the right granted to every human by virtue of free-will to either express or repress his Divine nature, but patience suggests, in addition, the expectation that at some point the individual will justify his or her existence by doing the *right* thing. Thus tolerance and patience must be inseparable. It is confidence in the other's essential goodness and integrity—the hallmark of tolerance—which endows patience with the assurance of a positive resolution.

Both tolerance and patience have a Divine prototype associated with the aforementioned doctrine of contraction. When God withdrew His Infinite Light to make space for creation, He left a latent impression (*reshimu*) of that light in the vacated space. This hidden impression is the Divine energy that is the foundation of all matter.

There is no aspect of creation that is not sustained by the infinite goodness drawn from within this impression, which the Ba'al Shem Tov called the "light that sustains all reality."[11] As such, the impression of God's Infinite Light suffers the negative character of material reality. By virtue of its connection with the pure essence of that reality, it evokes the affirmative spirit of tolerance associated with the *sefirah* of wisdom—the wisdom that impacts consciousness.[12]

When God withdrew His Infinite Light to make space for creation, the resulting impression set the stage for the subsequent introduction of the single ray of Divine light (*kav*) into the vacated space, or void (*makom panui*).[13] This ray of light, which originated in God's Infinite Light, penetrated into the center of the impression. As the light whose purpose is to illuminate and thereby rectify material reality, the ray of Divine light is identified in Kabbalah with God's *immanent* aspect—His presence in the world—even though it originates in the absolutely *transcendent* Infinite Light.[14] This paradox accounts for the possibility of finite creation rectifying or refining itself to such a point that it radiates God's infinite spirit.[15]

In penetrating the impression at the center of the vacated space of creation, the ray of Divine light is influenced by the spirit of tolerance, adapting it to its own design for creation and translating it into a force of patient endurance. It is this patient endurance that is considered one of God's thirteen attributes of mercy.[16] God is "slow to anger" (*erech apayim*),[17] patiently enduring the limitations of physical reality—chief of which is its potential for evil—while waiting for it to realize its Divine potential.[18]

Our expanding consciousness, and the tolerance that it implies, testifies to our belief in the eventual restoration of the Divine image that crowns our own super-conscious vision of reality. In its implicit acknowledgment of the Godliness embedded within every detail of creation, an expanding consciousness enables us to embrace differences while seeking to reveal the oneness underlying all.

Stability of Consciousness

Once the self has embraced conscious experience, meaningful interaction with creation can begin. The spiritual force that enables our consciousness to advance toward an active involvement with the particulars of our surroundings is channeled to us through the *sefirah* of understanding (*binah*).

Pure understanding expresses itself as that power of intellect that transforms the intuitive flash of wisdom into a mature thought. When expressed in the realm of consciousness, this power serves to steer us toward an appreciation of the complexity of creation—a complexity that engages the abstract sensibilities of our soul in an infinite variety of ways.

This process helps bring consciousness to a state of stability (*yishuv hada'at*, literally "the settling of consciousness," see also endnote 3), whereby an accommodation is achieved between the transcendent self and the *particulars* of outer reality.

Expansion of consciousness was seen above to be analogous to the Jewish People entering the "good and wide" Land of Israel. We may continue this analogy by noting that bringing consciousness to a state of stability entails the same psychological maturity and readiness that was necessary in order to settle the land (again, the Hebrew term for this stage in the unfolding of consciousness literally means settling).

Successful settlement that leads to stability requires that we first cultivate an identification with the particluar plot where we are about to take root. Only by acknowledging and appreciating the wealth of detail that the land encompasses can we focus our attention on the individual lines that radiate from the land's spectrum. Then we are ready to choose our individual portion in the land—to establish a personal relationship with it. Similarly, consciousness reaches stability when we can choose a spouse (or a vocation), from a broader field of potential choices—the wide expanse of land that we have already become familiar with as a result of the expansion. This maturity and readiness is what is meant by conscious stability (*yishuv hada'at*).

One way of imagining the first three stages of the unfolding of consciousness—its deepening, expansion, and stability—is through the following metaphor:

- in the depth of consciousness, we force our conscious self to "shut its eyes" as it were, in order to commune with our super-consciousness, our soul-essence

- having replenished itself at the fountainhead of super-consciousness, our conscious self reawakens—it "opens its eyes"

- in the initial expansion of consciousness, when our surroundings are not yet in focus, the self admits all the light of outer reality in equal measure

- finally, we can focus on our surroundings, as the self becomes oriented to specific elements of outer reality through the process of settling of consciousness

Unlike expansion, wherein we indiscriminately embrace a broad field of outer reality, stability allows us to inhabit individual components of that outer reality. The primary motivator for this is the soul's need to confirm the interdependency between all elements of creation. We do so by locating correspondences between the inner landscape of the soul and objective reality. In human relationships, for example, the element of consciousness associated with understanding helps us recognize character differences in people as reflections of God's creative design.[19] When two individuals encounter one another, a super-conscious harmonic is produced that can lead to a feeling of resonance.[20] Such resonance, when strong enough, is the prime indication that two people share a common destiny.[21]

Secure in our attachment to outer reality (by virtue of stability), we are free to interact with others, exploring their individuality without losing our own coordinates.

The earlier process of deepening makes an important contribution to this security, working as it does in unison with the process of the settling of consciousness. Both these processes exert a kind of anchoring force on the self: the former attaches it to its Divine source, while the latter grounds it within creation.[22]

Having imbibed the creative vision of super-consciousness, consciousness responds with keen sensitivity to the Divine underpinning of everything it encounters in the physical world. Maintaining this crucial connection, we are then free to explore reality in search of unique attachments through which we may realize our own essential character (as we shall see next).

3

Knowledge

The Core of Consciousness

Following the unfolding of the decision process we arrive at its core: the stage known as "the knowledge within knowledge" or the attachment of consciousness. Here consciousness becomes the hinge on which our soul's connection with outer reality depends. The nature of this attachment becomes the impetus for all of our tentative choices in life, choices that will ultimately be put to the test by active experience in the arena of knowledge and relationships.

Connecting with the reality outside ourselves depends on a selective attachment of consciousness (*hitkashrut hada'at*) to those elements in our environment that draw us the most strongly by virtue of a soul connection. As we shall see, marital relations—the union of two halves of the same soul-root—are described in the Torah as "knowing," which in Hebrew implies attachment (*hitkashrut*).[1]

While the routine work of consciousness demands the flexibility to continuously reframe our perspective, each individual attachment of consciousness to reality must be predicated upon an unconditional commitment to the pursuit of *integrated* experience—that is, experience that helps bridge inner and outer reality. Consciousness is the only tool we have with which our soul can probe the territory of experience, therefore, when the attachments we make prove unsatisfactory, we must make new choices that hopefully will produce a greater harmony between inner and outer reality.

But, our pursuit of integrated experience is not always guided by conscious thought. Many of our conscious choices emanate from the super-conscious realm. Although their subsequent refinement may be guided by elective thought, our initial attachment to a particular region of experience is definitely influenced by a hidden super-conscious factor.

To fully appreciate how the interplay between consciousness and super-consciousness expresses itself through these chosen connections, we need to explore the general nature of human will and its attendant capacity for choice, or as it is commonly termed: free-will.

Choice, Desire, and Drive

We have seen that the human capacity for choice is intimately connected with the power of the *sefirah* of knowledge in the soul. Insofar as this *sefirah* represents the ability to connect with and influence our surroundings, it follows that the capacity to make decisions is an essential hallmark of consciousness.

We have also seen that the very existence of a conscious life depends on the will of the self to break out of its super-conscious absorption within pleasure. The conciliation between pleasure and will—which is mediated by faith—signals the onset of consciousness and of its free-willed interaction with outer reality.

This is what provides the basis for all conscious decision-making. We can identify three manifestations of conscious free-will[2] that emerge within differing contexts:

- the first manifestation of free-will is termed choice (*bechirah*): the intellectual bond with some aspect of experience that engages the soul in a fundamental way[3]

- the second manifestation of free-will in conscious life is the sensation of desire (*chefetz*): the emotional longing for some form of gratification achievable only through outer experience[4]

- the third manifestation of free-will expresses itself most keenly in the drive (*ratzon*) of the soul to assert itself in its environment[5]: this expression of free-will is neither intellectual nor emotional—it is the instinctive and often inflexible force of raw self-assertion

All three manifestations of free-will that consciousness carries over from the super-consciousness come with some unseen mandates of their super-conscious origins. The conscious drive mirrors the super-conscious will, which is a drive toward self-expression that brings us from the super-conscious realm into conscious interaction with the world.

Desire reflects the influence of pleasure, pushing us toward outer experience for the sake of *inner* gratification.

Choice expresses our faith in the essential harmony between inner and outer experience. This deep-rooted conviction, which has its source in the uppermost reaches of super-consciousness, is what enhances our innate receptivity to outer reality, and enables us to identify those elements of the outside world that best evoke our inner ideals.[6]

To summarize:

origin in super-consciousness	form of free-will
faith	choice
pleasure	desire
will	drive

The differing origins within super-consciousness of these three forms of free-will are also reflected in the fact that choice is intellectual, while desire and drive are emotional and behavioral, requiring a connection with physical reality in an active way. This need expresses itself most powerfully in our drive to form external attachments in order to fill an existential vacuum.[7]

Inspired Choice

The degree of attachment to physical reality as expressed by any particular choice is determined by the degree of conscious focus that precedes it. By properly focusing on the relevant factors in a given decision-making situation, we can summon a new creative energy to break through what might otherwise seem like an impasse. Concentrated focus channels powerful spiritual soul-energies to decide to pursue goals that would otherwise appear outside of our grasp. By attachment of consciousness we begin to take hold of these goals.

Such inspired choice bears the imprint of transcendent faith. The hidden inspiration of faith most clearly asserts itself by helping us look beyond the obvious and identify the unique essence to which we are drawn.

Of course, not all choices tap the fountainhead of faith (as it were, faith does not automatically inspire our every decision). Most, in fact, involve no more than the resolution of different aspects of experience, and such simple choices do not introduce new energy from another realm. However, when faced with those critical junctures in life where we must make our most important decisions, only choice founded in faith can provide the kind of absolute resolve needed. These are decisions that invoke the deepest bonds between self and reality—such as, choosing a belief system, or choosing a marital partner, or choosing a vocation. In these situations, the path of faith is our only choice, as we learn from the Book of Psalms: "The path of faith I have chosen."[8]

This is the path, for example, that leads men and women to the mutual recognition of a transcendent bond linking their individual destinies. This recognition is then formalized through the decision to marry. Marriage—as a covenant eternally binding upon both parties—anchors a couple's commitment to each other in the spiritual realm of faith that inspired their initial choice. This guarantees that their love will survive the whims and vicissitudes of life.

Even as our super-conscious faith subtly influences such fundamental choices, the hard currency of consciousness must be taken into account as well. This is the significance of the two parallel modes of consciousness described earlier as higher-consciousness and lower consciousness. Each exercises its own form of attachment of consciousness, together with its own power of choice.

Higher consciousness represents the soul's approximation of God's own "knowledge" (or point-of-view). The great philosopher Maimonides defines God's knowledge in the following terms:

> The Holy One, Blessed be He, recognizes the truth of His Being, and knows it as it essentially is. He does not "know" with knowledge that is separate from Him, as we "know." We and our knowledge are not one; but for the Creator, He and His knowledge and His life are one from every side, every corner, and in every aspect of unification... It comes out that one can say: He is the Knower, He is the Known, and He is Knowledge Itself—all in one...[9]

Although our finite intellect cannot approach the absolutely unified knowledge of our infinite Creator, it can, by referring back to its super-conscious source, access the Divine wisdom from which our soul, and all of creation, evolve.[10]

Having done so, our finite intellect can re-focus our consciousness on outer reality and lead us to a level of knowing and a point-of-view that transcends ordinary human parameters. Though not to be compared with the absolute unification of God's own knowledge,[11] higher consciousness brings us as close as possible to a "pure union" with the objects of our awareness. In a male-female relationship, for example, "self" and "other"—sharing a common source in the Divine wisdom underlying creation—blend via higher consciousness into an integrated unit verified by faith and not by reason.[12]

This ultimate connection represents the supreme aspiration of consciousness. The inspired choice that makes this connection possible is that which we have already identified as emanating from the faith of super-consciousness via higher consciousness. As such, inspired choice represents the ultimate in free-willed determination.

The crowning achievement of higher consciousness in the history of the Jewish people was their acceptance of the Torah at Mt. Sinai. Together, the multitudes of Israel directed their choice heavenward and committed themselves to act upon and heed God's word as revealed in the Torah. The power to exercise their free-will in this way came from the Jews' having been chosen first by God. In fact, the first reference in the Torah to God's choice of Israel is in this context: "GOD, your God, has chosen you to be for Him a treasured nation, from among all the nations on the face of the earth."[13]

By choosing Israel, God invested the Nation of Israel with a corresponding power that enables us to this day to emulate the absolutely unconstrained freedom of choice that only He possesses.[14] This power of choice is reflected in every act by which we connect with God's transcendent will and the Torah that is its expression. It is this truly "free" will that allows us to introduce an entirely new, Divine energy into the created realm.[15]

Choosing Life

The quintessential choice asked of us by the Torah is the choice of life itself:

> Life and death I have placed before you, the blessing and the curse—choose life, so that you and your descendants shall live.[16]

Nowhere else in the Torah are we explicitly bidden to exercise our ability to choose. It would thus follow that some insight into the essential significance of choice might be gleaned by analyzing this unique command.

To choose life, in the literal sense, means to choose the eternal life of the World-to-Come (*Olam Haba*), which as explained in Kabbalah, is the "realm of souls" that exists beyond the past, present, and future. Although it can only be fully experienced once the soul has abandoned material existence, it secretly permeates all time frames.[17] Its influence in this world is felt by way of the energy it provides for spiritual renewal and transformation. By choosing eternal life in the here-and-now, we tap into the power to change our present, physical experience, as well as the character and meaning of life already lived.[18] Hence, it is a choice with far-ranging consequences.

On another level, the commandment to "choose life" could be read to imply that life itself is the consequence of a primal will, emanating from the uppermost reaches of the soul. Together, God and human beings join to create the wonder of life—not only as a biological event, but as a continuously regenerating product of their linked wills. Much as creation *ex-nihilo* recurs at every single instant, so conscious life is the result of our continuous re-creation of ourselves through the power of choice.

Although the essential power of free-will has its origin in the super-conscious realm of faith, its association with the existential imperative of choosing life is rooted in super-conscious pleasure—which introduces the soul to the joy of conscious experience in the physical realm.[19]

As noted earlier, it is the enclothement of pleasure within will that enables consciousness to ultimately override super-consciousness and become the dominant mode of human experience. And so it follows that it is in the conscious ability to choose life that we most keenly feel the influence of pleasure. This ability comes from higher consciousness. Lower consciousness, on the other hand, gives expression to the super-conscious influence of will, propelling us into consciousness in order to apply and actualize the ideals residing within pleasure.

These transcendent ideals, which are consciously affirmed through the power of free-will, provide us with the inspiration to confront the countless choices that present themselves in the physical realm. These are choices that are constantly being made by lower consciousness, which employs the conventional tools of human experience—

intellect, emotion, and instinct—in negotiating an interactive dialogue between the soul and physical reality.

Unlike the absolute choices of higher consciousness, these choices may allow two or more equally legitimate approaches; hence lower consciousness operates in a relativistic mode. Given a particular situation, lower consciousness attempts to identify the most acceptable position/action available. It does so by making value judgments—what is the "right" or "wrong" way to deal with the issues/factors unique to the situation. What we define as right or wrong in a certain business context, for example, will determine our choice of strategy in the situation.

But, these definitions cannot automatically be carried-over to a different moral context. Relativity, as a core tenet worked into the fabric of creation, posits our human morality with tremendously difficult questions regarding proper conduct in different situations. Therefore, we would like to devote some time to looking at the Kabbalistic and Chassidic frameworks for comprehending and undertaking moral choices correctly.

Clarifying Reality

The so-called moral relativity of reality serves a purpose. God worked relativity into the fabric of creation specifically so that we could clarify reality using the conscious faculties of our soul. Thus realitivity is grounds for granting us a mandate over reality. This mandate is referred to in Kabbalah as the work of clarification (*avodat ha'birurim*)[20]. As we have seen, lower consciousness is best suited to address this relativity, therefore, we are warranted to identify clarification (*birur*) per se as synonymous with the kind of choice exercised by lower consciousness.[21]

Just as the power of transcendent choice was bestowed on the Jewish people through their encounter with God at Mt. Sinai, the power of clarification was conveyed through the guiding principles that resulted from that encounter. The Torah provides the guidelines by which lower consciousness clarifies reality. This process began at Mt. Sinai and will end in messianic enlightenment, bringing with it a new state of consciousness that will identify the true Divine character of creation.

The process of clarification is predicated on the progressive differentiation of right from wrong at every juncture in life, hence it is essentially a process of "value" clarification.[22] The Hebrew word for value (*erech*) is also used in the Bible to denote comparison, as the Book of Psalms states: "None are comparable (*aroch*) to You."[23] While values are essentially relative and dependent on the context, this verse implies that this does not apply to God. In comparison to God, all other realities are absolutely insignificant, but in comparison to each other they are relatively significant.

Lower consciousness deals with relativity via two sensors: one that is sensitive to the good in reality, and the other to the bad.[24] These sensors provide the basis for two distinct yet complementary forms of clarification.

The first, known in Kabbalah as the clarification of "direct light" (*or yashar*) involves identifying the good and extracting it from the bad. The second, known as the clarification of "reflected light" (*or choʐer*), involves identifying the bad so that it can be separated from the good.[25]

In the first type of clarification, the sensor attuned to the good isolates that good so that the evil to which it is attached falls to a lower plane of reality. At this lower plane, a new aspect of good (undetectable as such on the higher plane) reveals itself. This requires another extraction, precipitating another fall, which results in the revelation of an even more subtle aspect of good. This process repeats itself until evil has fallen to its lowest level, at which point no further clarification or refinement is possible.

In the second type of clarification, the sensor attuned to evil isolates it from the good. Once released from its link with evil, the good rises to a higher plane of reality, where a new and heightened awareness succeeds in identifying a more subtle aspect of evil mixed in with it. Once that aspect is isolated and removed, the good again ascends, only to have the process repeat itself. Eventually, when all possible evil is negated, the good rises to its maximum height.[26]

Hence, we see that "good" and "evil" are relative values determined by the plane of reality that they occupy, and the sensor of consciousness that is used to identify them. The lower the plane of reality, the more subtle the good that consciousness seeks to clarify; the higher the plane of reality, the more subtle the evil. The further we proceed in either direction, the more refined our consciousness needs to be.

Ultimately, the caliber of our consciousness is determined by the degree of our success in distinguishing good from evil. The slightest clarification can elevate our consciousness to where a previously-identified good is revealed as a mixture of good and bad. This ongoing refinement proceeds with the aim of eventually distilling the ultimate good.[27]

Higher consciousness and lower consciousness work in tandem to help us achieve a complete rectification of physical reality. Rectification depends on clarification, and clarification, in turn, depends on the choices made by our higher consciousness, which transcends conscious experience, yet subtly guides it.

This interdependency of higher and lower consciousness—similar to the interplay of pleasure and will that initially gives birth to consciousness—accounts for the dual nature of most of the choices we make. Just as we cannot disassociate super-consciousness from consciousness, neither can we identify any single decision as entirely a matter of (super-consciously) inspired choice or conscious clarification. Higher consciousness and lower consciousness are forever entwined.

Tree of Life vs. Tree of Knowledge

The interdependence of choice and clarification—of higher consciousness and lower consciousness—is metaphorically illustrated in the Genesis account of life in the Garden of Eden, and the drama that revolved around the two trees that stood at its center—the Tree of Life and the Tree of Knowledge of Good and Evil.[28]

It is common to think of life in Eden, prior to the banishment, as that blissful state wherein man and woman lived in natural harmony with God's will.[29] This would, of course, imply a life void of consciousness and choice, and thereby render the miracle of existence irrelevant. But we know that life for the primordial man and woman was governed by both choice and responsibility. The responsibility came with the mandate to "work and preserve"[30] the natural realm into which they were placed, and the choice came from the command not to eat of the Tree of Knowledge.[31]

The dilemma facing Adam and Eve was one that would determine the path taken by humanity for all time—eternal life and blessing as already experienced in Eden, or "enlightenment" through knowledge of good and evil along with the curse of mortality it would bring. The two trees at the center of the garden that influenced their decision were the symbolic "counsels." (In Hebrew "counsels" are called *etzot* from the same two-letter sub-root as *etz*, meaning "tree.") God's command to refrain from eating of the Tree of Knowledge, which foreshadowed His later command to choose life,[32] provided the Divine standard against which they would have to measure that decision.

Prior to eating from the Tree of Knowledge, the first man and woman were perfectly objective in their assessment of outer reality, as their choices were free from the corrupting influences born of subjective experience. Their freedom from the distorting passions rooted in the knowledge of relative good and relative evil gave them absolute clarity. Or so it seems.

Nevertheless, Adam and Eve chose to embrace a consciousness dominated by mortality and the distortion of truth.[33] In short, Adam and Eve chose "subjective" consciousness over "objective" consciousness.

Given that Adam and Eve were commanded by God to make the right choice—"from the Tree of Knowledge of what is good and evil, you shall not eat, for on the day you eat from it, you will surely die"[34]—what could have led them to disobey God's revealed will? It must be that even in their pristine state, Adam and Eve were vulnerable on some level to the passions that would come to dominate human experience. Without such vulnerability, latent as it may have been, their obedience to Divine will would have been automatic. But, if any moral benefit is to be gained from free-will, there must be some tension between mind and heart, truth and passion—a tension depicted in the image of the first human beings poised between the Tree of Life and the Tree of Knowledge of Good and Evil.

When Adam and Eve ate from the Tree of Knowledge, they moved from choosing between absolutes (of super-consciousness) to clarification of relative values (of consciousness). Only then, did they experience free-will as a force capable of responding to distinctions of relative good and evil. The subjectivity they thus acquired enabled them to cultivate an empathy with the rest of creation, an empathy that would allow them to experience life from the perspective of physical reality.[35]

All of human choices ultimately come down to the two that Adam and Eve faced—the existential choice between life and death, between good and evil. For us, the two choices remain inextricably linked. The choice of life ultimately expresses itself through our inclination to do good, just as death is the consequence of our inclination toward wrong-doing.[36]

This amalgamation of "life and good, death and evil," placed before us at all times, suggests that the Tree of Life and the Tree of Knowledge share the same root. That they occupy the same space in Eden is implied in the verse in which they are introduced:

> And God caused to grow from the earth every tree that is pleasant to the sight and good for food, and the Tree of Life *in the middle of the garden*, and the Tree of Knowledge of Good and Evil.[37]

The implication that both trees grew "in the middle of the garden" is supported by a later statement from Eve:

> The woman said to the serpent, "From the fruit of the trees of the garden we may eat. But of the fruit of the tree that is *in the middle of the garden* God said, 'You shall not eat from it, neither shall you touch it, lest you die.'"[38]

That the two trees also shared the same root follows from the way their symbolic fruit (life and death, good and evil) are intertwined in the verse cited above.[39] Additionally, the *Zohar* calls the Tree of Knowledge of Good and Evil—the Tree of Death.[40] From this we learn that the Tree of Knowledge is nothing but the flip side—the back-side or shadow image—of the Tree of Life. In contrast to true, eternal life, the choices of lower consciousness between relative, subjective states of good and evil, belong to a life-death syndrome, which relative to true life, is considered death.

In our prayers we ask God "for life and not for death!"[41] Grammatically, the word "for death" (*lamavet*, not *lemavet*) implies "for *not* death." Thus, the prayer really reads, "for life and not for not death." We beseech God to bestow upon us true, eternal life and not to live a mortal existence that in truth is no more than a virtual state of "not death." Living a life of "not death"—void of conscious connection to the Torah, the will and wisdom of the Living God—is the relative, subjective good of the Tree of Knowledge of Good and Evil, the Tree of Death, the dark shadow of the Tree of Life that sprouts from the center of the garden together with it.

In summary:

Choice, as the initial transcendentally-inspired expression of free-will, is primarily an intuitive—and untested—product of consciousness not verified through experience. Hence, it must be subjected to the process of clarification, whereby it becomes a firm decision tested through experience.[42] Thus attachment, the central faculty of consciousness used in decision-making, occurs in two distinct stages.

The first stage reflects the influence of higher consciousness and involves the consolidation of the previous evolutionary stages:

- the initial re-immersion of consciousness, via the *sefirah* of crown, in its super-conscious roots

- its subsequent orientation to outer reality through its faculties of wisdom and understanding

- its bonding with that reality through choice

The second stage reflects the influence of lower consciousness and requires that the intellectual product of the first stage be drawn into an active relationship with the emotional forces of reality. The channels of clarification that allow this interaction between the "mind" and the "heart" of consciousness are those that we identified as the direct light and the reflected light. The coordination of these two channels of clarification is the focus of actual experience, as we shall see next.

4

Experience

The Bridge Between Mind and Heart

The ability to connect with elements of our experience—the essence of consciousness—is the key to the remaining chambers of the soul, wherein lie the forces of emotion and instinct.[1] These forces, which by their nature transcend logic, can nevertheless be harnessed in the pursuit of intellectual objectives. Indeed, their contribution is essential, as will become clear.

The soul seeks more than a merely theoretical connection with objects or ideas; it thirsts for union, because only through union can we confirm the essential compatibility between our innermost self and the universe. The act of attachment of consciousness provides the immediate impetus for this process. (Neither the expansion nor the stability that precede attachment have the power to elicit the total concentration needed to move the self into an animated pursuit of union with others.) Attachment creates a bridge between intellect and emotion and ensures a productive engagement of the self with the elements of the physical world through the forces of emotion and instinct.

Our emotional and instinctual makeup corresponds according to Chassidut with the *sefirot* of: loving-kindness (*chesed*), strength (*gevurah* sometimes translated as might or restraint[2]), beauty (*tiferet*), victory (*netzach*), thanksgiving (*hod*) and foundation (*yesod*). Each of these attributes affects a different stage in the advancement of the self toward its chosen connection with outer reality.

These *sefirot* and the emotional/behaviorist[3] reactions they ignite can be organized according to three basic kinds of psychological predilections, known as the right, left, and middle axes of the *sefirot*:

- **benevolence**: consisting of the *sefirot* of loving-kindness and victory, the forces of unchecked expansion, to the right

- **judgment**: consisting of the *sefirot* of strength and thanksgiving, the forces of restraint, to the left

- **mercy or compassion**: consisting of the *sefirot* of beauty and foundation, the forces of balanced expansion, the middle

attributes of judgment	attributes of mercy	attributes of benevolence
gevurah strength		*chesed* loving-kindness
	tiferet beauty	
hod thanksgiving		*netzach* victory
	yesod foundation	

Common to all these spiritual powers is the capacity to establish an interactive, feeling-based relationship between the self and outer reality. The powers of benevolence impel the self to seek a solid attachment with another. The powers of judgment, on the other hand, act with equal determination to restrain any such attachment. Ultimately, these opposing drives are mediated by the powers of mercy, which dictate the conditions under which a relationship with another can and should function.[4]

This native configuration of the soul demonstrates the inherent inclination of the self to invest its creative energies in the outside world.[5]

Of course, human beings do not always seek external attachments in order to affirm the truths of higher consciousness. In fact, we first pass through a period of immaturity, during which the emotional powers enumerated above dominate, while our cognitive resources—our internal wisdom, understanding and knowledge—remain virtually untapped.

This tendency of our immature consciousness to engage in try to clarify outer reality in an instantaneous and physically concrete manner often carries over into our adulthood, resulting in attachments and relationships that do not necessarily serve any long-lasting or spiritual objectives. Even when we are provided with certain absolute ideals through the choices made by our parents, teachers, or society, we are quite capable of sweeping these ideals aside when confronted by an onslaught of emotionally compelling distractions.

Knowledge does not proceed out of a vacuum. We do not clarify outer reality by simply falling under its influence. Only by testing reality against some absolute inner standard, can meaningful knowledge of both the self and others emerge.

In the search for a marriage partner, for example, this would imply that there must first be a clear understanding of what we need from an intimate relationship in order to fulfill our destiny. This understanding, which evolves in concert with other high-level choices regarding our mission in life, must remain the foundation of all life-defining decisions.[6]

Although the decision-making paradigm suggests that rectified choices should evolve out of wisdom, understanding, and knowledge, it is also legitimate for choice to originate in the intuition of the heart.[7] Indeed, while it may appear that consciousness is essentially a faculty of logic that co-opts emotion, its energy emanates from the intuitive interior of the heart, the super-conscious origin which ultimately influences the direction taken by the conscious mind.[8]

Such "knowledge of the heart" is crucial in helping us form a true image of others, rather than the one that is unduly influenced by the idealizations of our intellectual choice alone.

Empathy vs. Objectivity

We ended Chapter 3 with a discussion on the dual role that attachment plays as the endpoint of consciousness during its mental journey. But, just as knowledge, the *sefirah* associated with attachment, ends the mental half of the journey, knowledge also provides the starting point for its emotive half.[9]

As such, attachment gives rise to two opposite yet complementary emotive attributes of consciousness that play a decisive role in establishing a balanced relationship with external reality; these are: affinity (*kiruv hada'at*), associated with the *sefirah* of loving-kindness; and objectivity (*nekiyut hada'at*), associated with strength.

The literal meaning of the Hebrew idiom for affinity— *kiruv hada'at*—is "closeness of consciousness." Affinity implies a sense of feeling close to another, the same type of closeness shared with familial relations. When our consciousness is "close" to that of others, we naturally empathize with them; we participate with them, on the emotional plane in their varying psychological states of happiness or sadness.

In the decision-making process, affinity is the initial, spontaneous reaction of the heart to embrace the other, to choose the other in order to connect and unite with him or her. Affinity is figuratively described in the Song of Songs as: "his right arm embraces me."[10] The embracing right arm thus becomes the symbol for loving-kindness, the first of the emotive *sefirot* and the symbol of affinity, the first emotive stage of choice.

The opposite, but complementary, emotive *sefirah* and emotive attribute of strength (*gevurah*, also translated sometimes as might or restraint), is symbolized by the left arm "that rejects." In the decision-making process it is therefore identified as conscious objectivity. The Hebrew idiom for objectivity—*nekiyut hada'at*—literally means "purity [or cleanliness] of consciousness." The fear of blemish, of becoming impure or unclean, is what causes us to restrain ourselves from creating an attachment to another object or person until it becomes perfectly clear that it will not harm us in any way and, indeed, is exactly—objectively—the right one for us. Thus, objectivity is knowing, emotionally, how to keep a distance, how not to base one's decisions solely on the irrational, compulsive attraction of "love at first sight."

Though conscious objectivity stems from an emotive quality (just like affinity), it is more intellectually based. It can be thought of as "the mind within the heart" responsible for defining the parameters of the heart's outreach to contact and unite with outer reality.

It is important to note that each of these two stages of consciousness, if over exaggerated, can become obsessive. We may obsessively desire to embrace all, to choose everything and anything, without any concern as to what effect it might have on us. Or, we may become obsessively afraid to touch anything, to choose anything, lest it blemish us. To be productive, these two attributes—referred to in the well-known idiom "the left arm should reject and the right arm invite"[11]—must operate in balance.

Elegant Symmetry

Following loving-kindness (*chesed*) and strength (*gevurah*), the next *sefirah* that reveals itself in the soul is that of beauty (*tiferet*). In its purely emotive form, beauty denotes the emotional component included in the aesthetic experience and is the sensation aroused by the identification of elegant symmetry or harmony in creation. Consequently when taken in context of the decision-making process, beauty appears as the ability to appraise or weigh (*shikul hada'at*) options of choice. By means of appraisal we strive to judge[12] or balance our options by assessing their relative weight or value.

Appraisal exposes our inclination, first, to ultimately tip the scales of choice one way or another and, second, to move from a reflective to an instinctually active state. Rather than exposing just a "gut-based" decision, appraisal results from a complex process by which the derivatives of attachment, both those subjectively drawing us to any given choice (affinity) and those encouraging objective assessment (objectivity), are summed and measured against the prior idealization resulting from attachment itself.

The innate tendency of appraisal is to either identify a positive correspondence between the ideal and the available reality or, at least, to experience an indeterminate balance between the forces of affirmation and those of negation.[13]

Second, up to this point, the choice process has been predominantly reflective in its character. So, in addition to promoting a balanced assessment of potential, appraisal invites (if not demands) determination that can lead to decisive action. In the same way that super-consciousness impelled the self to take the quantum leap into consciousness, beauty inspires the transition from affective inclination to an instinctive determination that will characterize the choice process from this point on.

Instinct and Action

The *sefirot* of victory (*netzach*) and thanksgiving (*hod*) represent forces of emotive instinct and are responsible for spurring the soul toward decisive action in its pursuit of perceived objectives.

Victory is identified with the ability to overcome both inner and outer resistance to change.[14] The accompanying power of thanksgiving represents the opposing instinct—the soul's tendency to surrender to a higher force.[15] These two inclinations are described in Kabbalistic thought as forces of intuitive counsel preparing the soul for imminent, decisive action.[16] Although the inclination to surrender (identified with thanksgiving) might appear to undermine our resolve to act assertively, when coupled with the force of victory it actually promotes it by impelling those forces that resist change to yield to the overwhelming determination of our positive instinct.

Rabbi Yosef Yitzchak Schneerson, the sixth Lubavitcher Rebbe, offered the following analogy as a way to understand the respective effects of these two *sefirot*: the ability to overcome the immediate obstacles in our path derives from victory; the ability to hold our course through dedication to our intended destination derives from thanksgiving. In other words, while victory impels us to engage in active combat with *outer* forces of resistance, thanksgiving seeks to overcome *inner* opposition by nurturing our commitment to a particular goal.[17]

The states of consciousness that accompany this process are described in Chassidic thought as the states of resolve (*hachra'at hada'at*) and concurrence (*haskamat hada'at*).

These two powers of consciousness force a resolution of the quandary appraised in the previous stage of the process. Should the prior assessment of our experience fail to produce a dominant inclination to decide, the innate tendency of this aspect of consciousness will be to push for a positive determination.[18] The concept of resolution expresses the capacity of the *sefirah* of victory to vanquish the forces that resist affirmative change.[19] Nevertheless, should the relationship clearly hold no promise, this aspect of consciousness can just as resolutely promote a negative determination.

The force of concurrence, which complements the assertive drive of resolution, gives conscious expression to the power of surrender identified with the *sefirah* of thanksgiving. But thanksgiving acting alone, while capable of neutralizing our inner resistance to change, cannot convert that resistance into a force supporting decisive action.

Instead, concurrence acting in tandem with resolve, results in a whole-hearted acceptance of the decision that stands to be made.[20] The unanimous resolve of all our spiritual powers, achieved through the co-counsel of victory and thanksgiving, removes the final obstacle standing in the way of arriving at a definite decision.

Constructing New Realities

The name of the next power of the soul, foundation (*yesod*), intimates its role as the base upon which new realities are constructed through decisive action.

In terms of instinctive experience, the power of foundation is most closely related to what one might call the "creative urge"—a force of will with its source in super-consciousness, subtly shaped and influenced by the intervening forces of intellect, emotion, and instinct.[21] By the time this creative will is finally deposited into the sphere of foundation, it is already straining to actualize itself. Hence, foundation is depicted in Kabbalah as the most sensitive "organ" of the soul.

(In the anthropomorphic schematization of the *sefirot* employed by Kabbalah, the power of foundation resides in the sexual organ, responsible for executing the body's most primal creative impulse.[22] The position of that organ at the "conclusion of the torso" qualifies it as well to represent the fundamental power of foundation.)

The pressing urge to actualize itself through a constructive attachment to outer reality is what inspires the soul to act decisively. Hence, in Kabbalah this urge is known as the decisiveness of consciousness (*hachlatat hada'at*) or the power of decision. It is understood to imply the final forging of tentative and theoretical choice into a specific commitment to the world.

The crucial connection between choice and decision can be thought of in terms of the unique relationship between their corresponding sefirotic powers—knowledge and foundation.[23] The essence of knowledge has been described as a state of attachment to outer reality through super-conscious connections of the soul. The power of foundation, based on the same principle of attachment, seeks to translate those purely internal bonds into concrete actions that will yield results.

For example, the central decision in the realm of relationships is who to marry. The person one chooses serves as the focus of one's creative energies—the recipient of one's power of foundation. The decision to marry rests on a foundation of responsible and mature choices that come with adult consciousness. And arriving at the age of adult consciousness signals the maturation of one's decision-making powers as evidenced in the inclination to act with decisiveness.

This inclination reflects an innate force of goodness asserting itself in the soul. It represents the soul's determination to fight the destructive inertia that tempts us to abandon our free-will to random circumstance.[24] The tendency *not* to decide, even when seeming to be positively inspired, should always be suspect.[25]

The Joy of Deciding

The act of successfully concluding a decision brings a powerful surge of joy, the pleasure of being released from the clutches of doubt. Traditional wisdom has it that "there is no joy equal to the liberation from uncertainty."[26] This simple joy can itself often serve to ensure that the decision proves a blessing.

The joy that comes with actualizing the creative potential of foundation originally derives from the higher realm of the *sefirah* of understanding. In Kabbalistic imagery, understanding is characterized by the *partzuf* of *Ima*, or mother. Carrying this image further, understanding is described as the matrix from which emerge the remaining powers of the soul (loving-kindness through foundation)— thus, understanding becomes the "joyous mother of the children."[27]

Joy comes not merely from entering a state of motherhood, but from the experience of giving birth itself. With childbirth comes an end to the internal doubts and fears that occupy every expectant mother. In birth, there is finally certainty, and peace, and the joy of being released from the unknown. Such are the feelings that are re-awakened through decision-making, which gives definitive form to our tentative internal choices and which declares an end to uncertainty.

In addition to the joy drawn down from the realm of understanding, the decision-making power of consciousness releases a vital energy existing at the core of super-consciousness. The unique connection between super-consciousness and the *sefirah* of foundation, which comprise the two poles of the decision-making process, is evident in the tremendous vitality associated with the act of finally deciding. This vital force present in foundation is derived directly from the root of super-consciousness—the "essential lifeforce," that infinite well of Divine energy that is the source of all life.

To discover what we truly want in life, we must access the nuclear self that lies beyond consciousness. To achieve this end, we must tap the Divine energy that occupies the core of super-consciousness. That energy, when made available to foundation, supplies a force that is otherwise not available to consciousness. Hence, foundation inherits more than the cumulative energy of prior experience; it draws equally from the vital force inherent in the transcendent root of the soul.

Self-Expression

The actual act of decision-making is not the end of our journey; the ability to constructively express our decision is just as important and constitutes the final step in our analysis. Being able to properly explain our conclusions is evidence of having genuinely and completely examined their consequences. Regardless of whether the conclusion is positive or negative, an inability to communicate it testifies to a deficiency in the evaluative process. Thus, for example, difficulty in ending a relationship—as in the case of divorce—may be an indication of the need to re-examine and re-open the deliberations.[28]

The *sefirah* linked to the capacity for self-expression is that of kingdom (*malchut*). In Kabbalistic thought, kingdom represents the outer realm designated as the recipient of foundation's creative influence. By accepting and executing the sovereign will of foundation, kingdom provides a vehicle by which the abstract essence of foundation can express itself in ways otherwise unavailable to it.

This paradigm can be applied to our understanding of the relationship between God and creation, the soul and the body, man and woman, and any other dynamic relationship wherein the latter entity helps the former achieve concrete expression.

In accordance with this concept, we often find kingdom referred to as "the world of speech."[29] The power of the spoken word, which provides us with a way to express abstract thought or feeling, makes it a potent symbol for representing the power of kingdom in the soul.[30]

It would therefore appear obvious that this final stage of the evolution of consciousness manifests itself in the ability to verbally communicate the nature of our connection to the outer world. This function is referred to as expression of consciousness (*chavat da'at*) as in the verse from Psalms: "Day after day, uttering speech; and night after night, expressing knowledge (*yechaveh da'at*)."[31] The juxtaposition of the phrase "uttering speech" with "expressing knowledge" highlights the importance of verbalization in the revelation of consciousness.[32]

The Hebrew word for expression (*chavah*) is also the name given by Adam to the first woman: "And Adam called his wife's name Eve (*Chavah*), for she was the mother of all living being (*chai*)."[33]

One of the meanings of the two-letter sub-root of *Adam*—*d-m*—is "silence" (*dumiah* or *demamah*). The ultimate state of "silence" in consciousness is found in the highest of the crown's three super-conscious "heads," also known as the *Radla*, an ancronym-word that stands for "the unknowable head." Thus, the union of Adam and Eve implies the transition in the soul from silence to speech, from the beginning of consciousness (crown) to the end of consciousness (kingdom), with all the intermediate stages of consciousness contained within. And so we can better understand why the most all-inclusive decision of life is choosing a soulmate.

The relationship between the name Eve (*Chavah*) and "living being" (*chai*) intimates an important connection between the power of kingdom and that of foundation, the soul's most life-giving organ. Eve, the "mother of all living being," personifies the role of kingdom as the feminine repository of the vital life force (*chayut*) released through the masculine power of foundation.[34] If properly absorbed, this force becomes the essence of a new life, signaling the ultimate in actualization of self. This new life is nurtured through the maternal quality of kingdom, the fertile ground in which the formless seed of foundation takes root and grows. This function of kingdom is reflected as well in the verse that calls Eve the "mother of all living being."

The special relevance of Eve to consciousness is also apparent from the only other verse in the Torah in which her name appears: "And Adam knew (*yada*) Eve his wife."[35] This verse beautifully symbolizes Adam and Eve as the onset and culmination—the origin and repository—of consciousness. The properties of silence and speech expressed both etymologically and conceptually in Adam and Eve characterize the processes of deepening of consciousness (crown) and its expression (kingdom) that brackets the entire experience of the unfolding of consciousness.[36]

Proper self-expression enables us to communicate decisions from a position of serenity and strength. Nothing undermines our credibility more than a perceived inner-conflict, which we often expose in the way we communicate a decision.

The power of kingdom lies in its ability to persuade the potentially doubtful observer as to the appropriateness of our decision.[37] In order to accomplish this, we must express ourselves honestly and with proper regard for the integrity of the listener. If we do, understanding and acceptance of our decision should follow, even when perceptions differ.

Without the extension of kingdom, the inner truth of foundation cannot be adequately expressed in the outside world. Only after being absorbed by a living representation of that world (i.e., another human being), can such truths move us forward in the search for ongoing knowledge.

Summary

Thus far, we have examined the process of the unfolding of consciousness as paralleled in the *sefirot*. The stages that we have seen are: deepening, expansion, stability, attachment, affinity, objectivity, appraisal, resolve, concurrence, decision, and expression.

We will now see how this process works in the particular yet all-inclusive decision of life—choosing a soulmate.

PART II

Decision-Making
in Choosing a Soulmate

5

The Intimate Bond

Consciousness: Where Self Meets the Other

The unique relevance of the *sefirah* of knowledge (that is, consciousness) to the pursuit of human relationships is first made apparent in the Book of Genesis.[1] There, knowledge/consciousness is seen as the force binding Adam to Eve: "And Adam knew (*yada*) Eve his wife, and she conceived and gave birth to Cain, and she said: 'I have possessed a man before God.'"

The Biblical use of the Hebrew verb "to know" (*yada*) to connote marital relations indicates the central role played by consciousness in the consummate connection between man and woman. Here, the concept of knowledge appears divested of its usual meaning, expressing instead a kind of primal attachment to another that virtually eradicates the boundaries of selfhood. By depicting marital union as an expression of consciousness, the Torah is describing the essence of all true knowledge: a connection with someone or something outside the self. Few experiences evoke this as strongly as the intimate oneness with another human being.

Understanding consciousness as a connection clarifies the allusion in the above verse to a link between knowledge and possession.[2] When we own something, we incorporate it into our physical domain; when we know something, we incorporate it into our mental domain. Chassidic thought also sees an inverse implication—when we own or know something, we incorporate ourselves into it. In other words, ownership or knowledge involves investing our inner self into the object or idea we seek to own or understand.

Chassidic thought views the concept of possession as a process by which we enclothe ourselves within the acquired object.[3] Similarly, knowledge represents the process by which our consciousness becomes enclothed, or subsumed in the one we seek to know so that a union between the "knower" and the "known" can be achieved. This ability to unite is what makes consciousness the supreme facilitator of meaningful relationships.[4]

True Knowledge

The Biblical use of the verb "to know" (*lada'at*) in the sense of an "intimate union" is key to the understanding of consciousness in the *Tanya*, the seminal work of *Chabad*:

> Knowledge or consciousness is defined] as in
> the language [of the verse]: 'And Adam *knew*
> Eve;' that is, in the sense of binding and
> attachment. One attaches his consciousness in a
> strong and resolute bond and implants his
> thought firmly in the greatness of the Infinite
> One, Blessed be He, without the slightest
> diversion of consciousness.[5]

True knowledge implies union, the merging of the knower and the known at all levels of experience. Any lesser degree of knowing, though still a manifestation of other intellectual powers, lacks the total identification with the other that is the real aspiration of our consciousness. It is this sense of "intimate recognition"—which verifies the otherwise hidden super-conscious connection between the self and the other—that inspires all of our interactions with the outside world.[6]

In the passage quoted, Rabbi Schneur Zalman, the *Tanya*'s author, identifies how we can realize our highest potential consciousness, while averting diversions. Such success is dependent upon our incorporating into our consciousness the "greatness of the Infinite One." With this mindframe we are able to perceive not just the physical aspect of reality, but its *soul* or spiritual aspect as well. We are then capable of redeeming this spirit within all things and revealing the role that each part plays in the infinite array of Divine expression enclothed within creation. Being aware and attuned to reality as a unified totality is necessary in order to correctly assess our own role in relation to it.

Said another way, consciousness, like a reverse prism, is the medium through which we can channel the seemingly unfathomable diversity and even chaos of reality to our own center—our soul—so as to regain the unifying light of God's sustaining spirit to which our soul is connected. Such knowledge allows us to recapture the true image of reality and thereby achieve a lasting union with the universe we seek to "know" and "possess."

A Connection of Essence

The blossoming of the level of relationship associated with the pursuit of consciousness appears to be evident as well from another passage in Genesis[7] where God decides that "it is not good for man to be alone" and then presents Adam with an array of animals:

> And Adam conferred names on all the animals,
> the birds of heaven and the beasts of the field;
> and yet Adam could not find a helpmate to
> complement him."

The "conferring of names" alludes to a primary mode of expression of consciousness: symbolic objectification. Although Adam was successful in intuiting, conceptualizing, and expressing the essential nature of every living creature, he was still only able to "illuminate the other"—an understanding or appreciation that derives from lower consciousness.

The consummate form of relationship derives from higher consciousness and could only be forged with a creature who shared the Divine soul that set Adam apart from all other creatures. Such a relationship could only be achieved through union with Eve, as Adam proclaimed when she was finally presented to him:

> And Adam said: "This, at last, is bone of my
> bone and flesh of my flesh. She shall be called
> woman, for from man she has been taken."[8]

The fact that Adam apparently formalized his union with *his* other by naming her "woman" (*ishah*)—a word that both in Hebrew (and in English) is based on his own identity as "man" (*ish*)—tells us a great deal. First, he named her just as he named the other creatures,[9] indicating that an ability to identify or refer to our surroundings is a standard expression of consciousness. But, unlike other creatures, Adam gave his wife two names: initially he named her "woman" (*ishah*) but later following the primordial sin and its consequences, named her "Eve" (*Chavah*).[10] Being that the primordial sin is what motivates a second and distinct act of identification or reference, and that the primordial sin caused man to drop from higher to lower consciousness, we may conclude that there is a tremendous disparity between identity or reference (name) originating from higher consciousness (as the first name was) and that originating from lower consciousness (as the second name was). This disparity is great enough to warrant a second act of identification or reference, without which we may assume that it would have been impossible for Adam to fully relate to his wife.

To better understand how naming and reference as derived from higher and lower consciousness differ, let us consider two types of nouns:

- A proper noun derives from the relationship between the namer and the named. The essence of the named object or person can be identified by virtue of an affinity between the souls or spirits of the namer and the named. Thus, the proper name expresses the nature of the absolute union transpired by higher consciousness.

- A descriptive noun derives from the characteristics of the object or person

being named. Naming using a descriptive
noun is said to emanate from lower
consciousness, insofar as it identifies
symbolic characteristics that help the
namer establish a relationship with the
named.

Returning to our example of Adam naming his
helpmate twice: when Adam gave his helpmate her first name
he was responding to the realization that she was "bone of
his bone and flesh of his flesh," thus the first name,
"woman," reflects the assignment of a "proper noun."[11] The
fact that Adam included his own essence, man (*ish*) in her
name, woman (*ishah*), reflects the transcendent connection he
felt toward her that originated in his higher consciousness.

The second name that he gave her later, reflects the
lesser relationship of lower consciousness, and is clearly
descriptive of her relationship with the rest of creation:

> And Adam called the name of his wife Eve
> (*Chavah*), for she was the mother of every living
> being (*chai*)."[12]

We already examined in Part I Eve's special relevance to
consciousness and how beautifully Adam and Eve symbolize
the onset and culmination, the origin and repository, of
consciousness.

This Biblical allusion to consciousness as the hallmark
of any true relationship between man and woman beckons us
to explore the parallels between the pursuit of knowledge in
general and the particular search to know our "soulmate." In
the chapters that follow, we will re-examine the process of
the unfolding of consciousness in the context of a developing

relationship that allows a person to identify his or her marriage partner.

6

Singularity

Loneliness vs. Only-ness

Super-consciousness, by virtue of its transcendent nature, can be said to exist in a quintessential state of "singleness."

The singularity inherent in the super-consciousness (crown) realm is linked to the multiplicity of the conscious realm of our being via three strata of inner experience—faith (*emunah*), pleasure (*ta'anug*), and will (*ratzon*)—that, as we saw in Part I,[1] act as a bridge of sorts:

super-consciousness
faith
pleasure
will
consciousness

But the singularity of the super-conscious includes both a sense of only-ness descriptive of pleasure (pleasure here refers to the insular delight of the soul as it revels in its unique bond with God's Infinite Light) and a feeling of loneliness or solitude that drives will to identify with the finite realm (forming the bottom rung of the ladder connecting the super-conscious with the conscious).

Because of their inherently different, even opposite, expression of the singularity of the super-conscious realm, it is important that pleasure and will be balanced by faith. If not, their disparity may lead to an imbalance that can negatively influence our attitude toward relationships.

For individuals "free" of attachments, whose super-consciousness is dominated by the only-ness of pleasure, remaining single is essentially natural. Those who treasure the unlimited autonomy inherent in pleasure will find it hard to pursue any thread of attachment to the world around them, given the inevitable constraints that such attachments involve.[2]

At the other extreme are those "singles" whose super-consciousness is dominated by will and its tendency toward loneliness. For such individuals, the unattached state of pleasure—the necessity and ability to "enjoy one's own company," to "sing the song of oneself"—always threatens and must be avoided at all costs. In their desperate flight from solitude, they find themselves leaping from relationship to relationship. But such behavior can have the paradoxical effect of consigning a person to perpetual frustration and disappointment, since the absence of a properly balanced individuality will often undermine any attempt at forging a mature and lasting relationship.[3]

Both syndromes lead to a breakdown of the interface between the super-conscious and the conscious realms, thereby obstructing the process of deepening, the first step along the path of consciousness.

To correct these imbalances, we must seek to resolve the internal contradictions that lead us to deny either the self or the world. This can only be done by strengthening our faith.

Simple faith in the unity of all being is eternally imprinted on our soul and need merely be acknowledged in order for pleasure and will to harmonize. With the resultant easing of super-conscious tensions, the solitude of pleasure need neither be clung to nor feared, but accepted as an essential component of our will to pursue consciousness and relationship.

The Challenge of Being Single

The challenge of being single—the essential character of the *sefirah* of crown, our super-consciousness—lies in knowing how to wait patiently for the possibility of consciousness and relationship to present itself.[4]

In the Bible, the Hebrew word for crown, *keter,* has three meanings: as a noun, it refers to a "crown," but as a verb it connotes either the act of "encircling" (related to the crown's shape) or that of "patiently waiting," as used in the Book of Job: "Wait patiently a little while and I will show you."[5]

This verse from the Book of Job alludes not only to the inception of consciousness (within the *sefirah* of crown), but also to its completion (within the *sefirah* of kingdom). As we saw earlier, as regards the development of the decision making process, kingdom is associated with expression (*chavat da'at*).[6] *Chavah*, of course, is the Hebrew name of the first woman—Eve. If she represents the culmination of consciousness, then it follows that Adam must represent its initiation. In fact, the "deep sleep"—a state of super-consciousness—that God visited upon Adam, and out of which Eve was created,[7] is the quintessential symbol of the absolute silence[8] that precedes conscious expression.

Another indication of Adam's association with the *sefirah* of crown[9] is the Biblical implication found in the Book of Genesis that Adam was created with a dual gender:

> And God said: "Let us make man in our image, as our likeness; and they will rule over the fish of the sea...And God created the man in His image, in the image of God He did create him, male and female He did create *them*."[10]

The passage's alternating use of singular and plural lead the sages of the Talmud[11] to deduce that the first man was a being with "two personae" (*du partzufin*), one male and one female, symbiotically joined back-to-back. This interpretation is further reinforced by a subsequent verse, also in Genesis:

> This is the book of the generations of man. On the day that God created man, in the image of God He made him. Male and female He created them; and He blessed them and called their name Adam on the day He created them.[12]

From this verse it appears that the name *Adam* initially referred to two gender identities within one person; hence the impossibility of the first human being finding a partner.

After describing the first human being's failed attempts at identifying a helpmate, the Book of Genesis relates:

> And God caused a deep sleep to fall upon
> Adam and he slept; and He took one of his
> sides and then closed up the flesh beneath it.
> And God built the side that he had taken from
> Adam into a woman, and he brought her to
> Adam. [13]

Within the super-conscious state of the deep sleep, the male and female aspects of Adam's super-conscious self were sundered and allowed to face one another. This prefigured the splitting of Adam's physical self, signaling the creation of man and woman as independent biological entities.[14]

For Adam to awaken from his deep sleep and become conscious, the two poles of his super-conscious self (now separate) needed to re-unite (each within the other). This holographic merger was made possible as the force of faith inspired pleasure and will to acknowledge a shared identity.[15] This reciprocal alteration within Adam's super-consciousness allowed the first man and woman, once physically separated, to turn around and—whereas before their separation they had been back to back—to consciously reunite face-to-face.

In such a face-to-face relationship, each partner beholds his or her own image reflected in the other's eyes.[16] The holographic inter-inclusion achieved through this shared reflection produces in both partners a profound desire to reunite and thereby re-experience their common origin.

Every subsequent union of man and woman strives to fulfill the Torah's mandate of "and they shall become one flesh"[17] first realized by Adam and Eve in body as well as in soul.[18] The first couple's progression through the stages of symbiosis, individuation, and mature face-to-face reunion resulted in the human capacity for relationship that enables us to seek the translation of our super-conscious dreams into conscious reality.[19]

The Hidden Foundation of Love

The archtypal relationship between Adam and Eve best expresses the super-conscious connection we hope to achieve through marital union.

The initial Hebrew letters of their names—*Adam* (א) and *Chavah* (ח) spell *ach* (אח) meaning "brother," alluding to the fundamental fraternity (*achva*) of body and soul that the two experienced.

In the Song of Songs, the terms of affection used to describe the poem's lovers are brother and sister (*ach* and *achot*). The maiden is referred to by her beloved as "my sister" five times.[20] The maiden herself wishes that her beloved would be to her as a "brother," intimating her desire for the kind of bond that exists between those whose souls, like that of a brother and sister, share a common root:

> Were it that you could be as my brother, nursing
> at my mother's breasts; I would find you outside
> and kiss you, noone would scorn me.[21]

This plea expresses the desire to experience and display affection without any carnal shame. This state of fraternal endearment (*achvah*) is the super-consciousness foundation for love (*ahavah*). Unlike love, fraternity is constant and unwavering, anchored beyond the extremes of emotion that are so often characteristic of a relationship based on love.[22]

Stemming from the visceral realization of a common organic identity, fraternity reflects the unanimity-of-being experienced by the original man and woman before they were severed from each other.[23]

The initials *ach* (אח) derived from the primordial union of *Adam* and *Chavah*, are the first two of the three letters of the word "one" (*echad*) as in: "and they shall become one flesh."[24] Just as the physical coming together of Adam and Eve helped heal the psychic wound left by the sundering of their initial oneness,[25] so every union of man and woman seeks to revive the primal fraternal endearment that joins the roots of their souls.[26]

Waiting in Silence

One of the Hebrew words related to the name Adam is silence (*dumiyah*) alluding to the silence of our super-consciousness and the immobilization of consciousness.[27] It is an anticipatory silence, reflecting the soul's expectation of imminent redemption, as intimated in the verse: "For God alone, my soul waits in silence; from Him comes my salvation."[28] This salvation, in the case of human relationships, is the discovery of one's soulmate.

From within the mute realm of super-consciousness, the soul prepares itself for the work of consciousness by mirroring God's Infinite Light, the symbol of His creative will. This mirror function of super-consciousness is alluded to in the Torah's account[29] of creation: "And God said: 'Let us make man in our image, similar to our likeness.'" Having been fashioned in God's image, the human soul super-consciously mirrors the attributes of its Creator, serving as His facsimile, or "shadow," within the created realm.[30]

As God's *image*, the human soul passively reflects His will. As His *likeness*, the human soul actively adopts God's will as its own, emulating it through constructive, God-like activity.[31] The former function, which expresses itself through pleasure, facilitates the latter, but only after pleasure has merged with will.[32] As shown earlier, the purpose of the deepening is to spur our super-conscious faith to generate a face-to-face encounter between pleasure and will and bring about their union. It is this union that ultimately leads to a conscious recognition of the unrealized half of our super-conscious self—in the person of our soulmate.

Our soulmate is an essential element in our quest to establish the parity that is needed between super-consciousness and consciousness in order to recapture the Divine image of creation. For a man, whose super-consciousness is dominated by the abstract idealizations of pleasure, this means finding a woman who can cultivate his latent will to outwardly realize those creative ideals.[33] For a woman, whose super-consciousness is dominated by will and its over-identification with outer reality, it means finding a man who can help her reveal the hidden ideals that lie at the core of her own unrealized pleasure.

According to Kabbalah, a man's wife is a "parable" for what he spiritually aspires to in his engagement with the physical realm. A parable illuminates an abstract concept by cloaking it in concrete story form. Interestingly, the Hebrew word for "parable" (*mashal*) is related to the word for "dress" (*simlah*) and the word for "symbol" (*semel*), suggesting its function (which is also the function of a wife) as an intermediary between the abstraction of the soul and the concrete nature of physical reality. Nothing else expresses the sublime affinity between a man's innermost self and the rest of creation as does his choice of a mate, who provides the perfect model.[34]

As the figure interposed between himself and outer reality, a man's wife helps him process that reality and fashion his response. She is the "cloak" that expresses in its design the nature of his identification with God's will. He, on the other hand, represents the pleasure that she derives from modeling that will. Hence, he provides her with the reason for self-expression, while she provides him with its means.

The cloak of will is a cloak of light whose purpose is not to conceal but to reveal the otherwise invisible essence of super-consciousness that it enclothes by exposing it to consciousness. When that happens, the "light of will" becomes the "light of consciousness."

A cloak of light evokes the image of the verse: "[God] enwraps Himself in light, as in a garment."[35] This verse is interpreted as an allusion to God's Infinite Light that enclothes His essence, thus enabling God to assume an identity that created beings can relate to.[36]

Another allusion to a cloak of light can be found in the *Midrash* where Rabbi Meir refers to Adam and Eve's "cloaks of skin [עוֹר]"[37] as "cloaks of light [אוֹר]."[38] The commentators explain that Rabbi Meir wanted to thus describe the character of the garments prior to the eating from the Tree of Knowledge. One of the consequences of this sin—which is interpreted in Chassidic thought as a reenactment of the contraction (*tzimtzum*) of God's Infinite Light—was the condensation of the first couple's garments of light into the garments of skin. Hence, the two types of garment worn by Adam and Eve—light and skin—actually allude to the garments of super-consciousness and consciousness.[39]

In Kabbalah the cloaks of consciousness are called vessels (*kelim*) because they impose opaque boundaries upon the light (which would otherwise be blinding) so that it can be perceived by the self and others.[40] This light is perceived by the self through the vessels of intellect, i.e. thought. It is perceived by others through the vessels of character traits, i.e. speech and action.

The role of a wife in the physical world is to be a vessel for her husband. In this regard she is actually responsible for his achievements, though her role may appear to be merely supportive. Outside the physical world, at the level of super-consciousness, however, she is the true light of reality.

At the level of super-consciousness, the light enveloping a woman first attracts a man, for it is her light that will illuminate his identity. As for the woman, she is drawn to a man who embodies the hidden essence of her own motivation and desire. At the level of consciousness, their perspectives reverse. The man looks to the woman to create the boundaries for his creative potential. The boundaries of her vessel bring restraint and discipline to their life together. She in turn looks to the man for the light of benevolence to temper her native disposition toward severity. Hence, while she is now the vessel and he the light, their essential roles have not changed. She still seeks to promote self-expression (his and hers) while he seeks to revel in his Divinely inspired abstraction.

This process, though, must begin with the "expectant silence" of super-consciousness, achieved through the deepening of consciousness.[41] It is this silence that drowns the myriad and often conflicting voices that dominate our consciousness as we negotiate the challenges of life. Once these voices have been stilled, we gradually begin to discern a faint murmuring within—the "sound of subtle silence" that is the soul itself straining to be heard.

The "sound of subtle silence" is what the Prophet Elijah heard when God revealed Himself to him on Mt. Horeb.[42] The wind, quake, and fire, which came in advance of the revelation, and in which God was not found, symbolize the "sound and fury" of consciousness, which must abate before the calm "sound of silence" of super-consciousness.

The paradoxical association of "sound" and "silence" in this Biblical description of revelation suggests the origin of speech in the wordlessness of super-consciousness. Silence and speech are fused within super-consciousness into a rhythmic beat, like that of a drum, each beat producing the sound and the pauses in between producing the silence.[43]

The speech of our super-consciousness is the reflexive speech of the self in communion with the soul.[44] It is this voice of inner counsel, preparing us for the hard choices of life, which we solicit when retreating into the womb of super-consciousness. Once we have received it, there is no longer any reason to remain there.

The Divine imperative to leave super-consciousness and begin the work of consciousness is alluded to in the verse in Psalms: "God, do not silence Yourself; do not hush and do not be still."[45] We beseech God not to remain silent, not to remain invisible and inaudible to our senses, in a state of what for us is comparable to super-consciousness. We ask God to speak to us, to become conscious to us.

The extent to which our inner voice continues to reverberate within the chambers of consciousness determines the success of our search for knowledge and relationship.

The first of these chambers is accessible through the *sefirah* of wisdom where we experience the initial expansion of consciousness.

Expanding Consciousness to Include Another

The Talmud states: "A beautiful woman expands a man's consciousness."[46] The "beautiful woman" signifies the overall attractiveness of the physical world, beckoning us into consciousness so as to fulfill the Divine ideal of inhabiting the world.

This ideal to inhabit the world is encapsulated in the first commandment of the Torah: "Be fruitful and multiply."[47] Indeed, it is the basis for the continuity of life. However, its broader intention finds expression in the Book of Isaiah: "He did not create [the world] as a wasteland; He formed it to be inhabited."[48]

Of course, the way to inhabit the world is to have children, and it is the metaphorical "beautiful woman" who extends this invitation—into consciousness and into the physical world.

As human beings venture into the province of relationships, a vast spectrum of possibility presents itself. An expanded consciousness determines the range of individuals to whom we are super-consciously open and then admits the appropriate personalities into our conscious view.

While the hidden paradigm influencing the search for relationship derives from super-consciousness, the extent to which it is recognized and allowed to facilitate that pursuit is a function of influence of wisdom upon consciousness. The internal wisdom of consciousness is what keeps the window of consciousness open as wide as possible. Through the force of selflessness (which is its derivative), wisdom shifts the self from the center of consciousness, so that God's Infinite Light can penetrate the soul without interference and inspire genuine knowledge. It is this influx of light that expands consciousness. Selflessness then—together with its ability to nullify the ego—is the key to assuring maximum flexibility in relating to others.

Once we stand uniformly open to the diverse range of possibility for achieving interpersonal connections, the next power of consciousness—that reached through the *sefirah* of understanding—emerges to help us differentiate between particular individuals within that spectrum, allowing consciousness to properly "settle" or stabalize itself in outer reality.

The Talmud[49] describes a traditional courtship ritual that demonstrates the role of settling of consciousness (as defined in Part I) in helping us orient ourselves to the field of possibilities when seeking a soulmate. By contemplating the various accounts of this ritual, which we shall do in the next chapter, we can understand more fully how the fateful decisions of consciousness apply to human relationships.

7

Attraction

The Dance of the Maidens

In ancient times a biannual ritual would take place outside Jerusalem. The local maidens would form a circle and dance. The young men, gazing from a distance, would seek to identify the woman their heart desired. To improve their chances of being chosen, each of the young maidens would extol her prominent feature.

The *Mishnah*, quoting Rabbi Shimon ben Gamliel, relates:

> There were no days as festive for Israel as the 15th of *Av* and *Yom Kippur*, when the daughters of Jerusalem would venture out in borrowed, plain white garments (so as not to embarrass those who had none of their own) that were first ritually cleansed.
>
> The daughters of Jerusalem would venture out to dance in the vineyards, and what would they say? "Young man, lift up your eyes and behold she who is fit to be chosen. Do not set your eyes upon beauty; set your eyes upon family!"[1]

Elsewhere, the Talmud elaborates on this account:

The pretty ones among them, what would they say? "Set your eyes upon beauty, as a woman is for beauty."

Those with impressive lineage among them, what would they say? "Set your eyes upon family, as a woman is for children."

The unattractive ones among them, what would they say? "Take your acquisition for the sake of heaven so that you may adorn us with gold."[2]

This account is slightly amended in the compilation of Talmudic legends known as *Ein Yaakov*. There, a fourth category is added:

The wealthy ones among them would say: "Set your eyes upon those possessed of money."[3]

All told, four distinct reasons are given for choosing a particular candidate for marriage—beauty, wealth, lineage, and the sake of heaven.[4]

Together, these four categories can be understood to comprise the range of motivations causing a man to be attracted to a particular woman, or a woman to be attracted to a particular man.

Virtue, Pleasure and Profit

The Maharsha (the 16th century Polish Talmudist, Rabbi Shmuel Eliezer Edels) analyzes these motivators and suggests that by focusing on the aspiration that lies at the core of each they can be generalized to only three categories, in the following manner:

> Actions can be divided between those that aspire to virtue, to pleasure, and to profit.[5]

> The pretty ones are those who say that one should pursue the pleasurable.

> The ones with lineage say that one should be drawn after virtue (i.e., a good family).

> The unattractive ones say to pursue profit (i.e., the reward for choosing them, which can also be used to improve their appearance), as do the wealthy ones.

An apparent difficulty with the Maharsha's analysis is that virtue could also be identified as the reason motivating the choice of an unattractive maiden; as the Book of Proverbs states: "Grace is deceitful and beauty is vain; the God-fearing woman is the one to be extolled."[6] Additionally, taste for profit can motivate not only choosing the wealthy, but those with impressive lineage as well.[7] Thus, we would like to gain a deeper understanding into how virtue, pleasure, and profit do indeed constitute the primary underlying motivations at work in choosing a spouse and, following the Maharsha's commentary, how they relate to the four types of maidens.

To start, we need to keep in mind that an individual's attraction to a certain kind of person is reflective of much more than just "taste."[8] In choosing a spouse, we are not only declaring our commitment to another human being, but we are actively revealing our conception of our role and purpose in life. In its essence, choice of a marriage partner usually reflects our deepest attitude toward life and our expectations from it.[9]

In Chassidut, the source of attraction is identified with the super-conscious, where each individual's personal relationship with creation and God's creative power is manifest. We may recognize in the dancing "daughters of Jerusalem" archetypes for our relationship with God's creative design as a whole. Thus, all four archetypes taken together form, and correspond to, a model for the varying stages of the universe's design, as formulated in Kabbalistic thought. The central element of this formulation is the doctrine of contraction (*tzimtzum*) that was explained earlier.[10]

We will now examine how the successive transformations—that enabled the physical realm to emerge out of God's Infinite Light—are reflected in the attributes ascribed to the dancing maidens. It will become clear how each of the four archetypical maidens—the beautiful, the unattractive, the wealthy, the pedigreed—elicits a particular super-conscious response that expresses our identification with God's creative will and our desire to participate in its fulfillment. Furthermore, we will see how all four archetypes stem from the three motivators of attraction introduced by the Maharsha.

The Lineage of the Soul

> And the daughters of Jerusalem would venture
> out and dance in the vineyards. And what
> would they say? "Young man, lift up your eyes
> and behold the object of your choice. Do not

set your eyes upon beauty; set your eyes upon
family!"

As mentioned above, the contraction allowed a
seemingly empty void (*makom panui*) to be created, while the
Infinite light of God was held back, as it were, in the
backdrop to externally encircle and encompass (*or hasovev kol
almin*) this seeming void. The source of the collective soul of
Israel, the root of each individual soul, is identified in
Kabbalah and Chassidut with this Infinite Encircling Light of
God.

How does the collective soul correspond to the Infinite
Light? The answer relies first on the understanding that the
use of the term "light" to describe an otherwise
unfathomable force was meant to reflect its symbolic
significance, particularly of Divine goodness.[11] After having
created light, "God observed the light and saw that it was
good."[12] Likewise, the soul of Israel, by virtue of its sublime
derivation, inherits the benevolent character of God's Infinite
Light. This is reflected in the following statement of the
sages: "There are three characteristics to this nation [i.e., of
Israel]: being merciful, modest, and benevolent."[13]

These three characteristics are what accord the
collective soul of Israel its unique lineage,[14] alluded to in the
plea expressed by all the daughters of Jerusalem:[15] "Do not
set your eyes upon beauty; set your eyes upon family!" That
is, set your eyes upon the extended family of Israel, whose
daughters all share the lineage of God's Infinite Light.[16]

Courting Beauty

> The pretty ones among them, what would they
> say? Set your eyes upon beauty, as a woman is
> for beauty.

The contraction of God's Infinite Light through which God made space for finite creation is described in Kabbalah[17] as having occurred at the "center"—or the kingdom[18]—of the Infinite Light. The end result of the contraction process was the creation of a void in which finite matter was able to achieve a foothold. Through the selective re-introduction into that void of focused creative energy, God produces the succession of realms that culminate in our own physical reality.

Before undergoing contraction, the pure and undiminished energy comprising the kingdom of God's Infinite Light provides a field wherein God nurtures His aspiration for that which will be created. This Divine aspiration is alluded to in the first verse of the Torah: "In the beginning, God created [*eit*] the heavens and [*eit*] the earth." The definite article *eit* (אֶת) in the Hebrew original (which has no English translation) is numerically equal to "the aspiration" (*hashe'ifah*, הַשְׁאִיפָה), 401, referring to God's aspiration for heaven and earth, prior to their actual formation. As the Hebrew letters of *eit* also form the feminine pronoun "you" (*at*, אַתְּ), the aspiration to which the definite articles allude can be thought of as possessing a feminine character. In fact, the letters of aspiration permute into the phrase "beautiful woman" (אִשָׁה יָפָה).

The feminine character of the *sefirah* of kingdom in general is an essential element of Kabbalistic thought.

Kingdom is the receptive energy channel into which Divine lifeforce is deposited and then imbued with form. The womanly quality identified with the kingdom of God's Infinite Light stems from its role as the inspiration that both stimulates and sustains all of God's creative activity.

We can now interpret the statement of the pretty ones—"Set your eyes upon beauty, as a woman is for beauty"—as an invitation to elevate physical beauty to its source in the kingdom of God's Infinite Light so that it may serve to nourish our creative aspirations, just as the primordial core of God's Infinite Light inspired His own desire to create.

It is stated in Chassidic writings that there are those whose purpose on earth is to reveal God's enduring presence within creation through the beauty with which they are graced. In spite of God's apparent concealment, and the ruinous state of our own existence, we are beckoned by such beautiful souls to acknowledge the transcendent splendor that inspires creation and that remains as an unchanging and undiminished influence for all time.

Redeeming the Captive Light

> The unattractive ones among them, what would they say? "Take your acquisition for the sake of heaven so that you may adorn us with gold."

The purpose of the contraction was to provide a sheltered void in which finite being could evolve without direct contact with the blinding radiance of God's Infinite Light, which would otherwise annihilate all possibility of existence independent of Him. But, it was the creative potential within the core of that light that brought about the contraction in the first place. While the "pretty ones" reflect the splendor that reigned just before the light's withdrawal, the "unattractive ones" express the dark vacancy left in its wake. Their appearance, suggesting the blemish that the contraction left upon God's radiant countenance,[19] has an equally compelling effect on the soul.

The darkness of the void, which to our eyes seems to eclipse God's Presence, is reinforced by the seeming ugliness that so often characterizes physical reality. However, as explained in Part I, the void continues to retain an impression (*reshimu*) of God's Infinite Light. This impression, which survived the contraction, remains, to our eyes, the Divine basis of physical reality. As a remanent of Divine grace and nobility, it exists even within the darkest recesses of reality. Likewise, we may say that behind an externally unattractive face hides an inner beauty and grace that need only be acknowledged in order to radiate.[20] But, our ability to reveal the inner dimension of reality depends on the level of our own connection with that dimension within ourselves. The more alienated we remain from our own Divine source, the harder it is for us to discern nobility and grace in others and the more we see only ugliness and waste in its place.[21]

Initially it would appear, in line with the Maharsha's interpretation cited earlier, that the "unattractive ones" are trying to convince the young men to forsake the motivations that generally guide them in these matters, and instead seek the blessings that accrue from acting "for the sake of heaven" (*leshem shamayim*). However, interpreting their appeal in this fashion presents problems as it creates an inherent contradiction between the first part of their appeal—act for the sake of heaven—and the implied reward of the second part—expect material gain from your choice so that you might be able to adorn your wife with gold. Moreover, it does not leave us with any appreciation of how their most salient feature, "unattractiveness," might bring us to an appreciation of God's design for creation.

Hence, their plea must be interpreted more profoundly, as a challenge to the potential groom's consciousness, as if to say: "take your acquisition for the sake of heaven; that is, for the sake of the Divine Light itself, whose seeming withdrawal from the material realm is cause for our own unattractive appearance."

By embracing ugliness in the physical world, we affirm the ultimate Divine character of reality. It is a commitment that implies belief in the eventual revelation of God's Infinite brilliance (now only an impression) by means of creation, as we know it; thus, in a manner, releasing God from His own self-imposed exile.

Hence, the significance of the phrase "so that you may adorn us with gold." The Vilna Gaon (the 18th century Lithuanian scholar, Rabbi Elijah ben Solomon Zalman) suggests that the purpose of adorning a woman is to bring out her natural grace: "For grace is elicited through externals." Those externals—specifically, adornments—serve to amplify the intrinsic brilliance of the unattractive woman's soul, obscured by the impoverishing darkness of the contraction of God's Infinite Light.

By sensitizing our consciousness to the impression of God's Infinite Light trapped within physical reality and committing ourselves to its enhancement, we demonstrate an appreciation for the true beauty of Israel, which is but a reflection of the Divine aspect within creation.

Diversity and Unity

> Those with impressive lineage among them, what would they say? "Set your eyes upon family, as a woman is for children."
>
> The wealthy ones among them would say: "Set your eyes upon those possessed of money."

When God concealed His Infinite Light to make space for creation, the resulting impression set the stage for the subsequent introduction of a single ray *(kav)* of Infinite Divine light into the vacated space. This ray of light, which originated in God's Infinite Light, penetrated into the center of the void. This process entailed a series of constrictions of the ray itself and allowed for the evolutionary progression of created being from the purely Divine-like state to our own physical reality characterised in Kabblalah as the World of Action *(Olam Ha'asiyah)*.

With every constriction of the ray, a vessel *(kli)* was created whose outer "casing" *(chitzoniyut hakli)* derived from the energy of the impression of God's Infinite Light, but whose inner "soul" *(pnimiyut hakli)* came from the light of the ray itself.[22] As creation proceeded, the casings of the vessels became denser and the light that filled them became dimmer.

While the ray of light is ostensibly responsible for all the diversity within creation, its origin in God's Infinite Light means that it also suffuses all of reality with a spirit of Divine singularity. These two seemingly contradictory effects of the ray are identified in Kabbalah with its two dimensions:

- The "external dimension" of the ray is the force of differentiation that generates the rich complexity of being that camouflages the Divine oneness underlying all;

- The "inner dimension" of the ray, also called the string (*chut*) is a force of inter-inclusion that enables every element in creation to identify with every other, thus "weaving" them all into a single network.

These forces of differentiation and inter-inclusion, working jointly for the benefit of all creation, find expression respectively through those maidens of wealth or of impressive lineages who tout the unique advantage they can bring their prospective mates.[23]

From a linguistic perspective, the relationship between "ray," which in Hebrew literally means "line," and "lineage," is evident. The same holds true in Modern Hebrew where lineage is translated as *kav yochasin*, which literally means "a line of pedigree."

From a conceptual perspective, lineage reflects the force of inter-inclusion identified above with the inner dimension of the ray. The family line—immediate, as well as extended over generations—constitutes a network of hidden bonds and associations that influence us throughout life. Disparate individuals, separated by time, place, and temperament, impact each other's lives and experiences by virtue of their shared genetic makeup. The link joining these individuals mirrors a universal chain reaching back to the dawn of creation, which binds all humanity to one source and ultimately to one destiny.

As noted above, the singular appeal to lineage ("Set your eyes upon family!") attributed by the Mishnah to all the maidens equally, reflects the hidden root of all Jewish souls within God's Infinite Light, their ultimate source.[24] Those who can point with pride to their immediate lineage are really no more pedigreed than any other Jew, all of whom derive their spiritual essence from God's Infinite Light. Nevertheless, the fact that their lineage manifestly radiates that essence does lend them an advantage over those whose geneology does not. Such pride, however, is only justified if its purpose is to demonstrate to all Jews, regardless of current stature and lineage, how to cherish the legacy of their communal soul, which originates in God.

Thus, the suitor who would "set his eyes upon family" must exhibit a deep appreciation for inter-relatedness and inspire others to seek out the hidden connections that link us all into one great family of man.

In like manner, the suitor who "sets his eyes upon wealth" must elevate his taste for affluence by seeing the object of his desire as a model of God's desire—to endow creation with abundant resources for the sake of its own creative potential. As such, wealth represents the ray's external force of differentiation responsible for generating the manifest diversity of creation. Identification with wealth and rank demonstrates an affinity for the external, differentiated structure of reality.

Such an affinity need not undermine the root connection with the ray's inner force of inter-inclusion. It might even enhance that connection as long as the wealthy are consciously aware that it is the inner pulse of God's unifying energy that allows the multiplicity of creation to be generated through its outer dimension.

Insofar as the ray of light originates in God's Infinite Light, its outer dimension must convey some aspect of that source. The beneficent power of differentiation expresses itself through human consciousness such that, by mastering the complexity of creation, we can elevate each of its elements to its source in God.

In keeping with this analysis, we find that Jewish thought treats poverty and affluence essentially as states of consciousness, as suggested above by the Talmudic statement: "One is poor only in knowledge [i.e., consciousness]."[25] An affluent consciousness is one that is attuned to the incredible detail and nuance within creation, is aware of its Divine significance, and is desirous of sharing that appreciation with others. To the extent that the wealthy exhibit affluence in their consciousness, they can promote the force of differentiation, which sustains the unique and distinctive character of every element within creation.

As God's people in the world, Jews further His plan by mobilizing the material forces of creation in the service of His will, especially by providing for the needy. By dedicating our material resources to the alleviation of human suffering, we release not only the Divine power contained within those resources but, more importantly, the potential within the recipient otherwise frustrated by the constraints of poverty.

As every soul differs in what it needs to properly and fully express itself, the form that benevolence takes can vary greatly. It is the attention to individual differences that renders the act of giving more than just an outlet for compassion, but a force of redemption operating to release the unique potential within every element of creation. [26]

8

Decision

The Clarity of Choice

Choice, as the transcendentally inspired expression of conscious will, is primarily an intuitive—and untested—product of consciousness. Hence, it must be subjected to the process of clarification as verified through experience. Only then can it galvanize into a firm decision.[1] Let us now consider the relationship between choice and clarity as it applies to the pursuit of our soulmate.

As we saw from the Maharsha's explanation of the dance of the maidens, the conscious motivational factors identified with our tentative choice of a soulmate are: the desire for virtue, desire for pleasure, and desire for profit (or expedience). Insofar as our initial choice of a potential partner is super-consciously inspired, these three categories can be said to have corresponding associations with the three strata of inner experience that (as explained in Part I and above) act as a bridge between super-consciousness and consciousness: faith, pleasure, and will. Our choice of a marital partner is influenced by all three of these factors:

- Faith is the origin of our pursuit of that
  which is virtuous; it also inspires our

choice of religion or belief system, as such choices reflect the desire for absolute virtue in the form of the "essential good."

- Pleasure (in the super-conscious *sefirah* of crown) is the origin of our pursuit of that which is pleasurable; it also inspires our choice of a spiritual guide, usually picked for the "sweetness" of his light.

- Will is the origin of our pursuit of the profitable and expedient; it also inspires our choice of vocation, shaped by the practical considerations of what we do best and are most likely to succeed in and benefit from.

In Kabbalah and Chassidut, the woman is characterized as the primary magnet for a man's creative impulses and therefore is seen to embody all the values that he associates with the clarification of outer reality. That is why, in the story of the first man and woman, it was Eve who prompted Adam to eat from the Tree of Knowledge of Good and Evil. While Adam was apparently content to live his life in the protective shade of the Tree of Life—the source of eternal pleasure— his wife was drawn (as is will) to the expressive possibilities of a conscious life.

Once united in their choice, the first couple's banishment from the super-conscious realm of Eden was inevitable:

> And [God] banished man; and he placed the cherubim at the east of the Garden of Eden, and a flaming sword that turned every way, to

guard the path to the Tree of Life. And Adam
knew Eve, his wife...[2]

Before humanity can reclaim the Tree of Life,
specifically regarding marital relations, the apparent duality of
good and evil introduced through the fruit of the Tree of
Knowledge must be resolved. This process—the work of
rectifying creation in accordance with its Divinely intended
character—began with the relationship between the first man
and woman. However, in exile, the role of the woman does
not remain as it was in Eden. No longer the initiator of
choice, the female is a symbol—a parable (*mashal*)—for that
which inspires and helps clarify the conscious choices of her
spouse.

Applying this idea to the courtship ritual of the dancing
maidens described in the previous chapter, we should
recognize that though the role of choosing a marriage partner
is seemingly up to the young man who watches the maidens
from afar, it is nonetheless influenced almost wholly by the
will of the maiden dancing before him. Likewise, from earliest
times, Jewish law has prescribed that a woman can only be
betrothed in accordance with her will—the same will as that
of the lower consciousness into which mankind has entered
following the banishment from the higher consciousness of
the Garden of Eden.[3]

Expressing this same idea, the *Midrash* says: "Everything
follows from the woman."[4] A woman who is an exemplar of
goodness and integrity has the power to influence her
husband so that those become the qualities he is attuned to,
thereby strengthening his power of positive choice. On the
other hand, if the woman personifies wickedness and deceit,

she also has the power to lead her husband astray from the path of life and bring him to fatalism and despair—bereft of the will or desire to restore the Divine image to himself or his surroundings. Ultimately, Kabbalah and Chassidut perceive the wife to be the overruling impetus for making the choice of life.[5] She has the power to render his future one of life, should she convey the forces of good, or one of death, should she convey those of evil.

This is why in the Talmudic period in the Land of Israel, when standing under the marriage-canopy, the groom was asked: "[have you] found, or [do you] find"?[6] This seemingly unintelligible question alluded to the manner in which he had chosen his bride. Was it in the manner of the verse: "he who has *found* a woman has found goodness,"[7] or its converse described by the verse: "I *find* more bitter than death the woman whose heart is snares and nets, and whose hands are shackles."[8]

This last verse is the counterpoint to another that identifies the female in a relationship as the inspiration for choosing life: "See life with the woman whom you love."[9] In the Bible the verb "to see" oftentimes connotes positive choice, in the sense of "seeing" something as being fit for a commendable purpose.[10] Thus, the exhortation "to see life" in this verse actually mirrors the Torah's command to "choose life,"[11] or to see life positively. The addendum to this prescription—"with the woman whom you love"—points to the woman's role as the source of that optimism.[12]

This verse also encourages the husband to manifest his super-conscious pleasure—the pleasure derived from "seeing/choosing life"—through the will of his wife. This is tantamount to merging his power of choice with her power of clarity. The inspiration behind this union is the super-conscious force of faith that we have already identified as the origin of human desire for the essential good.

All in all, choosing a marriage partner then becomes a choice upon which life itself is predicated. Therefore, the selection of a spouse must emerge from the super-conscious root of the soul as a choice that transcends reason. Nevertheless, as choice can only be verified through the negotiation of real-life relationships, it must also avail itself of the powers of clarity associated with the woman and consciousness.

As noted earlier, consciousness operates in two directions. It transmits knowledge back and forth between the mind and the heart in the ongoing clarification of outer reality via the direct light (which is generated by the mind in order to illuminate the world) and the reflected light (which is absorbed from outer reality by the heart).

Since the direct light illuminates others with our own consciousness, it is the reflected light that must provide a control, verifying that there is true correspondence between that illumination and the character of the other we seek to relate to.[13] While both these energies operate in every human being, the tendency is for the direct light to dominate the male consciousness and the reflected light to dominate the female consciousness.

Although she embodies clarity in its entirety—both that associated with the reflected light of lower consciousness and that of the direct light of higher consciousness—it is particularly the clarity of the reflected light with which woman is identified.

While direct light reflects higher consciousness and its masculine force of optimistic idealism, it is the innate pragmatism of the reflected light more closely associated with the feminine that provides realistic feedback. It is this feedback that guides relationships to maturity and thus determines whether tentative choice will evolve into a consensual decision of both parties.[14]

In men, the male consciousness of the direct light manifests itself through the tendency to identify positive potential in others. Left untempered, this tendency makes it hard for a man to achieve an absolute commitment to any single woman, for new potential is always being identified among those who remain after he has made his choice.

Women reach a decision with greater facility. A woman's tendency as she proceeds through the successive stages of clarification is to identify the increasingly subtle defects of a relationship, until she is faced with one relationship whose positive potential is impossible to deny. Hence, the emotive force associated with the feminine side of the sefirotic chart (the side of restraint) expresses itself in the woman's tendency to hold herself back from identifying too closely with others. It is this initial guardedness that allows a woman to experience the absolute surrender to relationship, when finally faced with a man she comes to trust.

For a man to instinctually overcome those forces that oppose identification with a single woman, he often must overly invest himself in a relationship, in line with his power of benevolence in keeping with the masculine side of the sefirotic chart (the side of expansion). This, however, does not immediately lead to the exclusive and absolutist decision; rather, it is the concurrence of the woman, whose commitment to the relationship is much more singular and focused, which leads to a committed decision on both their parts.

It is important to keep in mind that these "male/female" responses are merely descriptive of generic proclivities that exist in all individuals. They are not formulae that can serve to define the exclusive roles of men and women in forming relationships. Indeed, a certain degree of role reversal can manifest itself in the course of time. This tendency is seen in Kabbalah as a harbinger of the Messianic Era, when the universal force associated with the female, will ascend above its male counterpart and initiate a new order in creation. Such is the hidden significance of the verse: "A woman of valor is the crown of her husband."[15] That is, a woman is the true ruling force in creation.

9

The Dating Process

The Pendulum of the Heart

The idealized image of our soulmate derives from the pristine choice corresponding to the stage of attachment (see chapter 3) associated with the *sefirah* of knowledge, but this choice must be subject to real-life tests and verification. The stages of consciousness that accompany the journey—from choice as it resides in the mind's eye to an actual decision—correspond to the levels of consciousness identified within the remaining *sefirot*:

sefirot	stage of consciousness' evolution	development of relationship
loving-kindness	affinity	dating with openness
strength (restraint)	objectivity	dating with objectivity
beauty	appraisal	assessing the encounter
victory	resolve	affirming the assessment
thanksgiving	concurrence	modifying objections
foundation	decision	reaching a conclusion
kingdom	expression	communicating the decision

We will dedicate this chapter to the dating process and to the role that the development of our consciousness has in forming our choice.

One point to keep in mind (that will be explored fully in the section dealing with appraisal) is that each successive stage reflects a maturation of the relationship at hand. Since not every relationship advances to the final stages (as many do not make it past the appraisal stage), we will treat the first three stages (affinity, objectivity and appraisal) in greater length. Affinity and objectivity are also the most utilised of all our emotive powers (both in terms of time and emotional investement) during the dating process, thus deserving of more in-depth treatment.

But, though we are keeping with our model here of the development of consciousness, it is crucial to remember that in reality things do not always comfortably follow a flowchart. Rather, what follows should serve as a constant reference, or material for recurring meditation, during (and before and after) each date, or each relationship. As such, it should help us recognize and adjust our more general bearings as to what our position and expectations are in relation to the fulfillment of our desire to get married.

Affinity and Objectivity

Our initial contact with a potential soulmate, usually in a dating situation, arouses a mixture of two basic dispositions founded upon the fundamental Kabbalistic forces—the *sefirot* of loving-kindness and strength (or, restraint). In interaction between self and other, each of the soul powers that pass through the mediating *sefirah* of knowledge (or consciousness) register as either a force of loving-kindness, bestowing consciousness with an expansive and obliging posture, or as a force of strength, generating discipline and restraint.

These two pivotal states of consciousness, which color every transaction with the objective world, are expressed by the affinity of consciousness and the objectivity of consciousness.[1] In the context of an inter-personal encounter, these two states render our experience with another either one of empathic identification or restraint and impartiality. These two modes of interaction are usually experienced simultaneously in varying degrees of combination. As we have seen earlier, the sages[2] refer to such a mixture as "the left [arm] pushing away while the right [arm] draws near"—a statement that reflects the Kabbalistic association of strength with the left arm and loving-kindness with the right.

Absolute and unchecked empathy can lead us to unconditionally bestow goodness on another without regard for the appropriateness or desirability of doing so. This can cause a relationship to degenerate; the receiver is either corrupted by a constant showering of undeserved affection, or forced to reject it in a desperate attempt to free him or herself from its suffocating embrace. Such rejection is a direct product of our natural resentment of having our individuality denied.[3]

Without objectivity, the urgency to achieve an empathic affinity with another can obliterate rather than affirm the uniqueness of the other. Maintaining a critical distance in a relationship ensures that we will properly absorb the other's reflected light and accept the crucial feedback that ultimately leads to a mature sense of affinity between two people. Objectivity's shielding effect should be viewed as a constructive element in the responsible pursuit of a relationship—predicated, as it must be, upon respect and consideration for the individuality of every human being.

In the context of a relationship, the proper use of both emotional resources of loving-kindness and restraint can generate important responses in the other. A concentrated attempt to keep oneself emotionally open and accessible helps produce a similar response in the person we are seeing, as does the attempt to maintain a posture of emotional restraint, corresponding with the famous verse: "as water [reflects] the face to the face, so the heart [reflects] a person to another person."[4]

Although our behavior in a relationship should not be consciously contrived to elicit certain responses, important lessons can be learned by seeing how the other person reacts to natural cues. Character is often demonstrated by the way a person handles the oscillating emotions produced in the course of a relationship. For example, it is worthwhile to observe if approval arouses joy or conceit, or if the alternative, disapproval (or rejection), inspires humility or anger. The way in which a person handles feelings of rejection can be as telling as the way in which he or she responds to acceptance.[5] The humbling terrain of abortive relationships often prepares us for the heights of joyous union, as expressed in the verse: "The humble shall increase their joy in God."[6]

When empathy and objectivity are properly harmonized, the inter-personal encounter produces an effect referred to in Kabbalah as touching and not touching (*mati velo mati*).[7] The sense of touching is elicited by making contact with another human reality. The emotional immediacy (and affinity) that attends such an encounter—measured by our own reactions as well as by those of the other person—creates a sensation of having broken through a wall of isolation. At the same time, as we empathetically merge with another's reality, the natural boundaries that separate the two selves intervene (through objectivity) to produce a sense of not-touching, of being unwilling or unable to achieve a complete connection. This sudden assertion of boundaries, as the two seek to both retain and consolidate their separate beings, demonstrates the profound need to preserve our individual identity.

The important thing to remember is that objectivity is not meant to supplant empathy. The key to maintaining a productive interaction with another person—one that will hopefully become an accurate determinant for a relationship's potential—lies in balancing these two tendencies as much as possible. This implies a need to compensate for our natural propensity toward one mode or the other. Individuals who lean toward prematurely bonding with others must work on cultivating their objectivity, while those with a natural tendency toward keeping a distance must work at cultivating their empathy.[8]

There is an additional aspect that affects the modulation of empathy and objectivity, and that is the extent to which we invest the other person's words or actions with meaning. Just as most individuals possess a natural tendency to either engage or hold back in a relationship, so too they can display a tendency to attach too much, or not enough, significance to another's words or actions. Attaching too much significance leaves little room for the other person to later challenge those impressions; this tendency undermines the formation of close attachments. The opposite tendency would seem to promote greater ease and lightness and foster the growth of such bonds.

But, of course, there can be other effects. Distance, initiated through objectivity, can sometimes afford the opportunity to view the other from a more balanced and forgiving perspective, in fact, promoting intimacy. Similarly, the growing attachment initiated through empathy and affinity can make us lose our natural ease and begin attributing disproportionate negative significance to things we see in the other person.

Unbalanced oscillation between affinity and objectivity creates a cycle of approach and retreat wherein sustained empathy eventually frightens us into the withdrawal posture of objectivity, paradoxically restoring the attraction by widening the distance and lessening the fear. But, when regulated properly, this cycle can help bring a relationship to a healthy balance.

Appraisal

Once equilibrium is achieved between affinity and objectivity, the relationship should ideally be sustained long enough for each side to compare the internalized image of the other (produced by the reflected light of each) to the prior idealizations of consciousness (produced by the direct light). At that point, the couple can come to a proper appraisal of the relationship's potential.

From the Divine point of view, not every meeting of another for the sake of finding our predestined soulmate demands that we acquiesce immediately. That is to say that by itself the simple fact that we are dating someone should not make us believe that it is a Divine decree that we are meant for one another. Rather, from the Divine point of view every meeting (even those that are unsuccesful) are necessary for bringing our consciousness to full maturity by the process that unfolds when we judge and appraise each proposal; all this before we are presented with the right one. Indeed, the sages teach that when in doubt, "sitting and refraining from action is preferable."[9]

Nonetheless, when we are in doubt regarding the potential of the relationship, we should allow ourselves to be open and sensitive to experiencing the finger of God pointing toward a specific choice.[10] This is an experience of the *sefirah* of beauty that reflects Divine Providence at play. In Kabbalah, the *sefirah* of beauty—which in our context corresponds to the next developmental stage of appraisal in consciousness—is understood to tend to the right.[11] What this means is that beauty should normally be seen as a "positively" leaning force. Applying this to dating situations, we say that, if after one's initial appraisal of the pros and the cons of a given relationship, it is hard to come to a decision—that is, "cool-headed" appraisal cannot come to a verdict—then the overall beauty of the encounter must be taken into consideration. One must try to become sensitive to the Divine Providence—as reflected by the circumstances *surrounding* the encounter—at work during dating. Sometimes, the frame of a picture significantly enhances its essential but quiescent beauty.

Resolve and Concurrence

At this stage, the two counselors of the soul in making the final decision come to play. They are the *sefirot* of victory and thanksgiving that correspond with the conscious powers of resolve and concurrence of consciousness. Resolve applies to the ability to affirm our positive assessment of the situation, while concurrence refers to the ability to modify or reform our initial objections based on that assessment.

When our power of resolve is victorious in saying yes to our positive assessment, it becomes the mandate of our *sefirah* of thanksgiving, which can also be translated as acknowledgment, to bring our consciousness to fully accept the "majority rule" of the soul's powers. Objections to the positive decision, based upon objective shortcomings one sees in the other, or subjective ill feelings with regard to him or her, must be overcome for the relationship to work.

To overcome an objection does not mean doing away with it completely, but rather modifying or shifting its weight in the overall assessment. In light of the positive elements and points of compatibility one experiences in the other, seeming negative characteristics or points of incompatibility become of minor significance in face of the whole. The totality of our relationship should identify with the majority of our impressions of the other side. The preponderance of positive impressions that make up the essential whole should outweigh and sweeten the relatively few negative ones.

The nature of the *sefirah* of thanksgiving or acknowledgment in this manifestation is to allow us to recognize truth that is beyond the scope of our rational mind.

Thus, concurrence here promotes the sense that be it as it may, this is my true *beshert* (predestined soulmate). At this point we foresee living happily with our spouse-to-be, trusting that our love for one another will not only conceal our weaknesses and shortcomings from the eyes of our beloved, but that our love will bring us closer to each other on all levels of consciousness, thereby strengthening our characters and healing our spiritual deficiencies. Our match is from God, and as God is the absolute good, only good will come from our marriage.

Decision and Expression

We now come to the last two stages of the dating process: decision, or reaching a final conclusion, and expression, which refers to the ability, and manner in which, we are to communicate our final decision.

The first commandment in the Torah[12]— "Be fruitful and multiply"—provides the context in which the *sefirah* of foundation expresses the most primal creative need of a human being. This need, originating in super-consciousness, can best be described as the need of life to bear life. Super-consciously connected to the essential lifeforce, it is felt as an overwhelming urge to share its power and blessing with another.

Every decision aimed at forging a constructive relationship with reality brings a release of the lifeforce hidden in our super-consciousness. However, the final decision to forge a relationship for the purpose of bequeathing new life draws down an altogether transcendent force of creative energy that is otherwise inaccessible. In contrast to the natural realm, the spiritual realm allows for the introduction of entirely new energy with every additional soul produced through the commandment of "be fruitful and multiply."

By drawing from super-consciousness down to its very foundation (in the *sefirah* of foundation) we can realize the most ineffable aspirations of the soul. The decision as to who we will collaborate with in bringing new life into this world certainly has to represent the peak of our exercise of consciousness.

All that remains is for that decision to be communicated to, and accepted by, the person at its focus. The ability to fully express our decision to the other, and thereafter to make our decision public, is the final stage in the evolution of consciousness and relationship in dating. Before it is verbally expressed, the decision is not yet finalized.

A rectified soul is one that is true to his or her word.[13] Thus, to express one's desire to marry borders on making a vow, an oath of faithfulness, to one's spouse-to-be. An oath, like a covenant, engenders hidden, super-conscious powers of the soul.[14] The final *sefirah* of kingdom, corresponding to speech, is embedded in the primal *sefirah* of crown, that is, in the super-consciousness.[15] The timeless, eternal super-conscious thus becomes manifest in speech.

With the verbal expression of our decision to marry we begin to embrace our spouse-to-be on the spiritual plane. In the Talmud, speech is used as an aphorism for marital relations.[16] If, as the Ba'al Shem Tov teaches, willful thought places us "where we think,"[17] how much the more so when our thoughts find expression in words of desire and commitment.[18] "Words spoken from the heart enter the heart."[19]

With our spoken words of love and desire to marry we bring our decision into the world. As every Jewish home is a "miniature sanctuary,"[20] we can now begin to fulfill our life's work of creating, on earth below, a home for God.[21]

Supplementary Essays

1

Consciousness and Knowledge[1]

In Biblical Hebrew, *da'at* implies both knowledge and consciousness.[2] In Modern Hebrew, the term used for consciousness is *muda'oot* (מוּדָעוּת), which stems from the same grammatical root as "to know" (יָדַע). Incidentally, this is also the case in English, as the word "consciousness" etymologically stems from the Latin for "knowledge."

Though the derivation of the Modern Hebrew term is late, it does allude to a particularly meaningful Biblical grammatical issue. Grammatically, *muda'oot* is in the passive *hofal* form, a form that appears *only three times* in the Bible: twice in the context of one becoming conscious of his sins,[3] and once in the context of God's greatness becoming known to the entire world.[4] The numerical value of this last verse

זַמְּרוּ הוי' כִּי גֵאוּת עָשָׂה מוּדַעַת זֹאת בְּכָל הָאָרֶץ

is 2370 and is equal to 5 times that of knowledge (דַעַת), 474, a phenomenon which, as we shall see, alludes to the complete manifestation of Divine consciousness inherent in the *sefirah* of knowledge.

As will be explored later, in Kabbalah knowledge is viewed as bipolar: masculine and feminine. The more active state of consciousness, implied by *da'at*, is generally identified with male

1. See p. 1
2. As in Deuteronomy 4:42.
3. Leviticus 4:23, 28.
4. Isaiah 12:5.

consciousness, while the more passive state, implied by *muda'oot*, is generally identified with female consciousness. Of course, as we are referring to a conceptual mode of male and female, in actuality, both men and women may manifest male and female consciousness (with one or the other being predominant in the personality).

Building on the conceptual link between these two terms—*da'at* and *muda'oot*—we find that they are also linked numerically. *Da'at* (דַעַת) equals 474; *muda'oot* (מוּדָעוּת) equals 526; their sum is exactly 1000, alluding to the consummate revelation of Divinity described as the one thousand lights God gave Moses with the Torah at Mt. Sinai.[5]

Since their sum is 1000, the average value of the two terms is 500, which is equal to the numerical value of the words "Be fruitful and multiply"[6] (פְּרוּ וּרְבוּ), God's first and all-inclusive commandment to mankind. In the Torah the verb "to know" is used in the sense of conception and procreation. The numerical distance from the average value to each of the two particular values of *da'at* and *muda'oot* is 26, the value of God's essential Name, *Havayah* (י-הוה), the Divine power that brings all reality into existence.

Muda'oot also equals *kan tzipor* (קַן צִפּוֹר), the "bird's nest",[7] which in Kabbalah connotes the spiritual chamber where the soul of the Messiah waits for God to command him to come redeem the world.[8]

---

5. Arizal's *Sefer Halikutim, Beha'alotcha.* *"Veha'ish Moshe."* See also *Likutei Sichot*, vol. 6, p. 245.

6. Genesis 1:28.

7. Deuteronomy 22:6.

8. *Zohar* II:8a.

The "bird" symbolizes the Messiah himself who will bring eternal peace to mankind.[9] Bird (צִפּוֹר) has the same value as peace (שָׁלוֹם), 376.

The nest symbolizes the Messiah's relatively feminine, receiving state of consciousness, and as such can be understood to represent the Messiah's spiritual soulmate. Nest (קֵן) is gramatically cognate with acquiring or possessing (קָנָן) knowledge (see also Chapter 5, endnote 3). Thus, the unfolding of consciousness is indeed the unfolding of the messianic potential inherent in creation.

---

9. Isaiah 9:6

2

Functional Levels of Knowledge[1]

Though in relation to lower conscisouness higher consciousness is relatively concealed, nonetheless both are considered revealed relative to two more levels of knowledge present in the super-conscious. Together, there are thus four levels of knowledge or consciousness in the soul that correspond to the four letters of God's essential Name, *Havayah.*

The *yud* (י) corresponds to the knowledge of (the *partzuf*[2] of) *Atik Yomin* (the Ancient of Days)[3] that connects the soul's essence to its super-conscious pleasure and will.

The first *hei* (ה) corresponds to the knowledge of (the *partzuf* of) *Arich Anpin* (the Long, Patient Face) that connects precognition—*mocha stima'ah* (the concealed mind) of *Arich Anpin*—with conscious wisdom.

The *vav* (ו) corresponds to the knowledge of wisdom or (the *partzuf* of) *Abba* (the Father)—extending to and including the foundation of *Abba*—that connects the intuitive mind of wisdom to the analytic mind of understanding.

The final *hei* (ה) corresponds to the knowledge of understanding or (the *partzuf* of) *Ima* (the Mother)—extending to and including the foundation of *Ima*—that connects the soul's intellectual and emotive faculties, or *midot.*

---

1. See p. 2.

2. The higher persona of the *sefirah* of crown.

3. Identified in Kabbalistic terminology as the knowledge of the crown's unknowable head, the *Radla* (see "The Three Strata of Super-Consciousness," p. 16ff.)

To summarize, let us present these four types of consciousness in chart form:

letter	consciousness		knowledge of	connects
י *yud*	concealed	higher	*Atik Yomin*	pleasure and will
ה *hei*		lower	*Arich Anpin*	concealed mind and wisdom
ו *vav*	revealed	higher	*Abba*	wisdom and understanding
ה *hei*		lower	*Ima*	understanding and emotive faculties

3

Between Intellect and Heart [1]

Although higher consciousness operates as the unifying force between the soul's intellectual faculties of wisdom and understanding (the male and female sides of the intellect), the process by which it does so is by first bridging, within wisdom itself, its purely abstract perception of reality and its measurement of reality. While pure perception (a selfless experience shining its light inwardly to the self) is wholly objective and remains intellectual, measurement entails sensing the relationship of the measurer to the measured. It thus possesses a subjective feeling of self toward the other, an emotive, outwardly oriented strain within the mind itself.

Knowledge also acts within the higher strata of our soul by transfering the experience of another being (as already manifest in our soul's ultimate essence to the relatively lower super-conscious pleasure and will that the soul feels toward that being) and subsequently connecting precognition with intellect. Even at these higher levels, knowledge first acts within the masculine side, connecting its "intellect" (its own relatively "male" dimension) with its "emotion" (its relatively "female" dimension), and only then links the masculine with the feminine half of the union. And so, knowledge may always be seen as poised midway between the intellect and the emotions, as depicted in Kabbalah.

As the intellect is an inwardly directed vector force, while the emotions are an outwardly directed vector force, both possessing real dimensionality and direction, they represent two opposite

---

1. See p. 3.

states of "something." For knowledge to connect them, it must incorporate a state of "nothingness," and like a non-dimensional point of convergence (*keren zavit*) it must have a twilight-like quality being neither and, at the same time, both of the two opposites it connects. For this reason, knowledge is usually not included as one of ten *sefirot*.

Here is another way to understand how knowledge is two things at once. The two levels of knowledge, higher and lower consciousness, are often explained in Chassidut to correspond to two different, opposite perspectives on reality. From God's perspective—higher consciousness—the world is envisioned as being created "nothing from [the true] something [i.e., from God]." In relation to God's absolute being, created reality (including the infinitesimal measure of His light and lifeforce by which He creates finite reality) is as naught.

But from our human perspective—lower consciousness—the world is envisioned as being created "something from nothing." We experience created reality as "something," while the Divine source of light and lifeforce that continuously brings it into existence remains unknown to our senses—"nothing." Between the two extremes of "being" exists a common "nothing" that connects them. This is the pivotal point of knowledge.

As noted, knowledge is the essential good of the soul. The words good (*tov*) and nothing (*ayin*) are strongly connected in Kabbalah. Numerically, good (טוֹב) equals 17 and nothing (אַיִן) equals 61. Together, they equal 78. Since each word possesses three letters, the average value of all six letters is 13, the numerical value of one (אֶחָד). One (אֶחָד) possesses 6 permutations. As above, good (טוֹב) plus nothing (אַיִן) equals 78, or the value of all 6 permutations, and hence each of their six letters may be seen to correspond to a particular permutation of one (אֶחָד).

If we take each letter of "good" and multiply it by the corresponding letter of "nothing" we get: ט · א $= 9$; ו · י $= 60$; and ב · ן $= 100$. The sum of this "particular multiplication" of the two words is 169 or 13^2. But, 13 is the value of one (אֶחָד), and so 13^2 is just "one times one," אֶחָד · אֶחָד—all is one!

4
Self and Other[1]

The dual nature of the self—that is, the soul—is expressed through the complementary terms "self" (*etzem*), implying introversion as in "for oneself" (*le'atzmo*), and "other" (*zulat*), implying extroversion as in "for another" (*le'zulato*).

"Other" (*zulat*) is linguistically related to "degradation" (*zilzul*), alluding to the self-abasement that is often necessary in order to leave the state of "for oneself" and devote oneself to another. The enigmatic verse: "as degradation [*zulut*] is exalted amongst men,"[2] may hence be read: "as one must lower his feeling of exaltedness [a feeling that derives from the solitary state of for-oneself] for the sake of his fellow men."

Another word that "other" (*zulat*) is related to is *nazal*, meaning "flowing down," descriptive of the Divine "sustenance" or "flow" (*shefa*) that emanates from on High. This word is also related to *mazal*, which although usually rendered as "fortune," literally means "a source of downward-flow." This etymological proximity allows us to envision the other as a recipient of the unending flow from the fountainhead of one's being.

The Jewish soul is blessed with the paradoxical character of being both self-possessed and other-obsessed. The initials of self (עֶצֶם) and other (זוּלַת) in Hebrew spell the word for "might" (עֹז), which is numerically equal to *mazal* (מַזָל). Extrapolating from the verse: "God shall grant might [עֹז] to His people; God shall bless

---

1. See p. 13.
2. Psalms 12:9.

135

His people with peace,"[3] we may say that the initials עז, of self and other, hint that a Jew's strength lies in his or her ability to harmonize self-interest with responsibility for others. In the same vein, might also appears in a verse that describes the capacity to love an other with all of one's might—even transcending the barriers of the self's physical life: "For love is as mighty [עַזָּה, from עַז] as death."[4]

---

3. Psalms 29:11.

4. Song of Songs 8:6.

5

Before Being Human[1]

A free fall into the domain of super-consciousness can represent a terrible threat to any individual. This is not a baseless fear. The realm of crown/super-consciousness when independent of knowledge/consciousness is characterized in Kabbalah as a state of chaos (*tohu*).[2]

In the song of *Ha'azinu*, the word for chaos refers to an uninhabitable and desolate realm: "[God] found [Israel] in a desert land; in a desolate howling wilderness [*tohu yelel yeshimon*]."[3] The "desert," or land of chaos, is characterized in the Book of Jeremiah as a "no-man's land": "[He] Who leads us through the desert... in a land through which *no man* has passed and where *no man* has settled."[4]

As the inner realm of chaos, where God's Infinite Light obliterates all sense of self-ness, crown represents the no-man's land of the soul. As such, it stands in contrast to the territory of knowledge, from where man begins the work of "settling the world."

By analogy, the derivative crown of the *partzuf* of knowledge, which figures in the deepening of consciousness, is the non-human (*lo adam*—the idiom used to describe the Divine essence of Israel) within the human. Thus the non-human is like the core of non-

---

1. See p. 14.

2. See *Etz Chayim, Heichal Abiya.*

3. Deuteronomy 32:10.

4. Jeremiah 2:6. See also I Samuel 15:29, where God Himself is referred to as "no man."

identity within the self wherein all the raw creative energy absorbed through the super-conscious encounter with God's Infinite Light is stored. However, it serves only as a temporary retreat from consciousness whereby one can draw down the inspiration necessary to continue the pursuit of a meaningful and productive relationship with outer reality.

6

The Seven Inner Senses[1]

When the seven forms of creative energy isolated by pleasure are enclothed within the executive power of will, they manifest as seven inner senses (*chushim*). This happens by way of what is known in Kabbalah as the seven rectifications of the skull (*zayin tikunei gulgalta*), upon which all other rectifications of reality depend. Each rectification (*tikun*) of the skull inspires an inner sense. These inner senses are the primary arbiters of consciousness—that is, they determine the character of every individual's consciousness, as well as the way in which each one of us responds to outer reality.

Rabbi Hillel of Paritch, in his commentary on Rabbi Dov Ber Schneersohn's *Sha'ar Hayichud*, explains the role of these inner senses as follows:

> The rectification of consciousness is dependent upon one possessing an inner sense for the essence of the thing he is trying to apprehend. For example, the one who is benevolent by nature—in the very core of his soul—is the one whose kindness (the ideal experienced through pleasure) serves as the source of his will. Hence, this source generates within him a continual revelation of the will-to-do-good. This revelation, nevertheless, remains super-conscious.

> The attachment of self to the essence of a thing, as experienced in will at the moment one exercises one's will, is referred to as an inner sense. The inner sense then elicits a

---

1. See p. 17.

derivative attachment of intellect (merely an extension of the essence), such as a rationalization of the necessity to do works of kindness, or a contemplation of the numerous pretexts for bringing kindness about. The depth of one's intellectual attachment is directly proportional to the depth of one's inner sense (attachment of will) for the thing's essence.

7

The Land of Israel[1]

While the phrase "a land flowing with milk and honey" appears often in the Bible in reference to the Land of Israel, the phrase "a good and wide land" appears only once, in the first reference to the Promised Land in God's words to Moses.[2]

The numerical value of the Land of Israel (אֶרֶץ יִשְׂרָאֵל), 832, equals 32 · 26 (the value of both heart, לֵב, and glory, כָּבוֹד, multiplied by the value of God's essential Name, *Havayah*). The value of the Land of Israel is also equal to the numerical value of the phrase light-of-the-crown (אוֹר הַכֶּתֶר), the super-conscious enlightenment of the soul.

The phrase "a good and wide land" (אֶרֶץ טוֹבָה וּרְחָבָה) possesses 12 letters. Starting with the 1st letter (*aleph*), skipping 4 letters to the 5th (*vav*) and 4 more to the 9th (*reish*) spells אור, the word for light. If we treat the phrase as circular (the last letter linked back to the first) we can skip 4 more letters to the 13th, which would then be the first *aleph*, and so on. Thus, the word "light" continues to appear and re-appear in the phrase endlessly, alluding to God's Infinite Light,[3] the light revealed in the soul's super-conscious crown. God gave the Land of Israel to the People of Israel in order to reveal this light in their collective consciousness.

---

1. See p. 24.

2. Exodus 3:8.

3. The numerical value of infinite (אֵין סוֹף) in Hebrew is itself equal to the numerical value of light (אוֹר), 207!

"Good," "wide," and "flowing with" correspond to the depth, breath, and length of consciousness respectively, as described in the words of Rabbi Hillel of Paritch quoted elsewhere.[4]

---

4. See Chapter 2, endnote 3.

8

Tolerance and Patience[1]

While in its literal sense slow-to-anger (*erech apayim*) is a single attribute, in Kabbalah it is interpreted as two traits: *erech* and *apayim*. This can be explained in line with the distinction between tolerance and patience: *erech*, which literally means length or extension, alludes to the indefinite extension that is manifest in tolerance; *apayim*, on the other hand, connotes anger, the element that makes patience tentative as in the Midrashic expression: "He extends His anger, but collects that which is His" (*ma'arich apei v'gavi dilei*). This interpretation clearly demonstrates the need for tolerance in one's soul before assuming the more critical posture of finite patience.

The numerical value of *erech apayim* (אֶרֶךְ אַפַּיִם), 352, is equal to that of "milk and honey" (חָלָב וּדְבַשׁ) in the oft repeated description of the Land of Israel in the Torah as "a land flowing with milk and honey."[2] This equality indicates that the Divine attribute of *erech apayim* manifests especially in the Land of Israel. In our homeland, God is especially tolerant and patient with us and we are to be especially tolerant and patient with one another. We noted above that "flowing with" pertains to the length of consciousness, the understanding within each level of consciousness. Indeed, the word *erech* means length. While the source of the attributes of tolerance and patience, *erech apayim*, lies in the super-conscious crown, they first appear in consciousness as

---

1. See p. 27.

2. Exodus 3:8, 3:17, and more.

the length (understanding) of wisdom, the expansion of consciousness.

9

Choice and Intellect[1]

The identification of choice (בְּחִירָה) with the intellect is supported by the fact that by a slight permutation of its letters in Hebrew it becomes "God has chosen" (בָּחַר י-ה).

This alludes to the verse: "For God [י-ה] has chosen Jacob for Himself, Israel for His treasure."[2] Jacob symbolizes the serious student of Torah, while his name Israel (יִשְׂרָאֵל) permutes to spell "I possess a head" (לִי ראשׁ) implying intellectual brilliance.[3] In Kabbalah, the two letters of the Divine Name in this verse, י-ה, refer to the two Divine intellectual faculties of wisdom and understanding.

The numerical value of the Name י-ה is 15. The numerical value of choice (בְּחִירָה) is 225, which equals 15^2, and like all square numbers, implies a state of perfect inter-inclusion, in this case of all the particular powers of the intellect.

A square number in general implies *intellectual* perfection, for the goal of intellect in its contemplation of any aspect of reality is to perceive (with wisdom) and grasp (with understanding) the presence of every part of the whole in each of its parts. And so, if the whole consists of n initially visible parts, the goal of intellect is to reveal its n^2 details. With this in mind, by taking the product of the numerical values of the five letters of the word choice (בְּחִירָה), ב · ח · י · ר · ה $= 2 \cdot 8 \cdot 10 \cdot 200 \cdot 5 = 160,000$, which is also a perfect square, 400^2. 400, itself the square of 20, is the numerical

---

1. See p. 33.

2. Psalms 135:4.

3. Arizal's *Likutei Torah*, *Vayishlach* 32:29. See also *Derech Mitzvotecha* 15b.

value of the last of the 22 letters of the Hebrew alphabet, the letter ת (*tav*). 400 is the numerical value of the word that means "source of intelligence" (מַשְׂכִּיל). Through in-depth contemplation, one ideally arrives at 160,000 details—from which to choose!

10

Will-power[1]

The word will (רָצוֹן) in the sense of will-power or drive, is cognate
in Hebrew to the the word for running (רִיצָה). Running is a
function of the legs, which, in Kabbalah, correspond to the two
primary instinctive powers of the soul, victory, and thanksgiving.

The common two-letter sub-root of will and running, רצ, can
be seen to stand for "running" and "marching" (רִיצָה צְעָדָה). The
first instance of running in the Torah is when Abraham ran to
greet guests.[2] The first instance of marching is when the daughters
of Egypt marched along the walls to catch a glimpse of the beauty
of Joseph.[3] Both reflect the instinctive drive to fulfill an existential
need of the soul.

The only time in the Bible that marching (צְעָדָה) appears as a
noun is in the account of King David waging war against the
Philistines. God instructs David not to attack until he hears "the
voice of marching at the top of the trees."[4] "The voice of
marching" refers to the voice of the angels of God marching at the
top of the trees to come to the aid of David and his troops. In
Kabbalah, the military and waging war relate to the instinctive
powers of the soul. Although marching appears in other contexts,
its primary reference is to the marching of soldiers in war.
Significantly, the numerical value of the phrase "voice of
marching" (קוֹל צְעָדָה) is equal to that of running (רִיצָה), 305. God

---

1. See p. 33.
2. Genesis 18:2.
3. Ibid. 49:22.
4. II Samuel 5:24.

continues His words to David that upon hearing the voice of marching on the top of the trees—"then attack!" The word for attack, *techratz*, ends with the syllable *ratz*, the root of *ritzah*.

The numerical value of running-marching (רִיצָה צְעָדָה) 474 is equal to that of knowledge (דַעַת), alluding to consciousness at the instinctive level of the soul, the conscious drive to fulfill existential needs. In Kabbalah, knowledge is understood to be the inner lifeforce of the soul's instinctive or behavioristic attributes—victory, thanksgiving and foundation. In particular, it is the wisdom of consciousness that serves as the lifeforce of the soul's intellectual faculties; the understanding of consciousness that serves as the lifeforce of the soul's emotive attributes; and the knowledge of consciousness that serves as the lifeforce of the soul's instinctive powers.

With regard to the decision-making process, the power and vitality of knowledge to influence decision comes to its forte in the three stages of the process that correspond to the instinctive powers of the soul; resolve (*bachra'at hada'at*, the victory of knowledge), concurrence (*haskamat hada'at*, the thanksgiving of knowledge), and decision (*hachlatat hada'at*, the foundation of knowledge). Here, one is actually *making* the decision.

11

God's Essential Choices[1]

The four instances of Divine super-rational choice can be seen to correspond to the four letters of God's essential Name, *Havayah*:

letter of God's Name	choosing of	*sefirah*
י *yud*	Priests	wisdom
ה *Hei*	Levites	understanding
ו *Vav*	Israel	knowledge
ה *Hei*	David	kingdom

Normally in Kabbalah and Chassidut, the three primary subdivisions of the Jewish nation into Priest, Levite, and Israel are seen to correspond to the *sefirot* of loving-kindness, strength and beauty. To explain this alternate correspondence we need to focus on additional traits of each sub-group.

Among the priest's (or *cohen*'s) primary functions in the Torah is the eye-witnessing of the leper's wounds to ascertain whether the leper is to be spiritually and physically quarantined. The power of sight, and especially the Biblical allusion to the power of spiritual healing inherent in the priest's eyes, relates the priest to the *sefirah* of wisdom, whose counterpart physical sense is sight.

Relative to the association of the priest's capacity with wisdom, the Levite corresponds to understanding. When describing the Levites duties, the Torah uses a peculiar phrase:

---

1. See p. 37.

"the Levite shall serve *he* the service...."[2] The seemingly unnecessary *he* in the middle of this phrase alludes to the *partzuf* of *Atik*—which in this case represents pleasure—awarded the Levite during his Divine service.[3] The pleasure originating in *Atik* is experienced in the "structurally" developed first *hei* (ה) of God's essential Name, *Havayah*, which corresponds to the *sefirah* of understanding.

Israel, the "mature" name of Jacob, is used as a generic appelation for a Jew who is neither a priest nor a Levite. As further explained in "Knowledge and Understanding" (p. 153), this maturity identifies the ultimate development of the *sefirah* of knowledge, or the ability to sense the Divine in Jacob's role as a patriarch. As such, it also designates the natural tendency of every Jew to "feel" his or her source in the Creator.

Finally, as the first king of the eternal monarchial dynasty of the Jewish people, David represents the *sefirah* of kingdom.

The sum of the numerical values of these four Divine choices, כֹּהֵן לֵוִי יִשְׂרָאֵל דָּוִד, equals 676 or 26^2. 26 is of course the numerical value of *Havayah*, God's Essential Name (י-הוה) to which we have just corresponded these same four. Thus, God's super-rational choice is revealed as self-referential; as if God were choosing His own "Self."

Though impartially we might think that a people and a king are necessary for the expression of the Divine at the communal level, we might wonder as to the necessity of priests and Levites. But, this numerical equality also reveals that were the priests or Levites missing, so would the self-referential element found in the super-rational essential choices made by God be missing. In fact, numerically, just כֹּהֵן לֵוִי together equal 121 or 11^2; 11 is the sum of the numerical equivalents of the last two letters—*vav* (ו) and *hei* (ה)—of God's essential Name. So in a sense, the priests and

---

2. Numbers 18:23.

3. *Zohar* III:178a.

Levites provide the "space" occupied by the ordinary Jews and the king.

(Note also that the value of the initials of these four sub-groups [כ ל י ד] is 64 = 8^2, another perfect square.)

12

The Linguistic Root of Choice[1]

The Hebrew root of the word "choice" is composed of three letters *bet-chet-reish* (בחר); the root letter *bet*, acts like the prefix letter *bet* that denotes the state of being-within; *chet-reish* can spell the word for hollow, or cavity (חור). Consequently, we may interpret the act of choosing as an expression of our desire to fill the "hollow" of creation—the void that was created after the contraction of God's Infinite Light and that defines our reality—with a blessed revelation of primordial Divine energy. In the same vein, choice may be seen as reflecting this very process at the personal level, whereby each individual seeks to fill his or her own existential vacuum with a consummate relationship with another.

The conceptualized relationship between the letters *bet* and *chet-reish* can be extended to two of the permutations of the root בחר: to-connect (חבר) and to-destroy (חרב). In the root בחר, the *bet* ("within") is merely facing the "cavity," thus implying the detached, yet anticipatory nature of choice's identification with outer reality. In the root חבר, the *bet* succeeds in penentrating the cavity, thereby alluding to the linkage with reality that follows one's *bechirah*. But, in the root חרב, the *bet* is figuratively turning its back on the cavity. This alludes to the destructive disassociation of one's self from creation and the loss of desire to attempt a genuine reconnection.

---

1. See p. 38.

13

Knowledge and Understanding[1]

The power of differentiation ascribed to consciousness derives from its close association with the *sefirah* of understanding. While the *sefirah* of understanding contrasts and compares elements in the realm of pure intellect, the *sefirah* of knowledge performs the same function in the realm of values. The affinity between understanding and knowledge is evident from the *mishnah* that states: "If there is no knowledge there is no understanding; if there is no understanding there is no knowledge."[2]

This is also evident from the blessing in the weekday *Amidah* prayer that reads: "You endow man with knowledge and teach the mortal understanding...." The capacity for differentiation that knowledge and understanding share, finds unique expression in this blessing, insofar as it is the blessing in which we insert the statement of *havdalah*, or differentiation, between Shabbat and the weekdays. The *Jerusalem Talmud*, in explaining why *havdalah* is inserted in this specific blessing, states: "If there is no knowledge, how can there be differentiation?"[3]

The combined numerical value of understanding (בִּינָה), 67, and knowledge (דַּעַת), 474, equals that of Israel (יִשְׂרָאֵל) or 541, which is read in Kabbalah as the two words לִי ראֹשׁ which mean "I possess a head." We may interpret this to mean that the "head," or intellect of Israel, consists of only the *sefirot* of understanding and knowledge, the powers of clarification and choice, because the

---

1. See p. 41.
2. *Avot* 3:17.
3. *Yerushalmi Berachot* 5:2.

sefirah of wisdom is above intellect in the normal sense of the term.[4] In the passage from the *mishnah* quoted above, understanding and knowledge are seen to be interdependent, while wisdom and awe are seen to be interdependent. Or, we may interpret the above *gematria* to mean that the innate intellect of Israel (understanding and knowledge) proclaims that "I possess a head" above my normative intellect—that is, the wisdom of the Torah.

---

4. See *Tanya*, chapter 18.

14

Clarification and Selection[1]

The two forms of clarification (*birur*) correspond to the two forms of selection (*breirah*) discussed with regard to the laws of Shabbat: "selecting the edible from the inedible" (corresponding to the positive clarification of the direct light) and "selecting the inedible from the edible" (corresponding to the negative clarification of the reflected light).[2] The former type of selection is permitted on Shabbat, while the latter is not—implying that as a "day that is all goodness," Shabbat represents an exclusively affirmative approach to clarifying reality.

The Hebrew word *bar* (בר), which is the two-letter sub-root of the root *b-r-r* (ברר), denotes "grain"—a food item that can only be obtained through *breirah*, by separation from its chaff. Its two component letters—*beit* and *reish*—are the core consonants found, respectively, in the Hebrew words for "love," אֲהַבָה (associated with loving-kindness) and "fear," יִרְאָה (associated with strength). Hence, they allude to the two "hands" of consciousness that execute clarity, each in its own fashion.

Both of these processes of clarification are alluded to in the Torah's account of creation. The first word in the Torah—*bereishit* ("in the beginning")—alludes to the initial clarification of the direct light, whereby God Himself (the ultimate good) is differentiated from the rest of creation: the *b-r* of *breshit* represents the process of *birur*; the *alef* of *bereishit* that follows represents the *aluf*, "supreme" Being and paragon of goodness, who is singled

---

1. See p. 42.

2. See *Shulchan Aruch, Orach Chaim* 319.

out; and the final three letters—the שִׁית ("six," in Aramaic) of *bereishit*—represent the six days of creation that "fell away" from God, initiating a new and inferior plane of reality.

The next word in the text, *bara* ("He created"), alludes—as a repetition of the בר and *alef*—to the successive clarifications (*birurim*) that transpire as the material realm sinks to its lowest energy level—that represented by the words *tohu vavohu* ("void and formless") in the second verse of the Torah. At this point, the *birur* of the reflected light commences in the guise of evolution, whereby higher species "rise" from lower ones, in the same manner as good continuously rises from evil.

Hence, creation can be viewed as a two-stage process of devolution and evolution, the former representing the descent of matter to its lowest existential state (the *birur* of the direct light), and the latter representing the ascent of spirit to its highest existential state (the *birur* of the reflected light).

15

Naiveté vs. Natural Consciousness[1]

Before the primordial sin, man and woman did indeed possess a state of natural naiveté. They were unaware of their nakedness, that is, unaware of the immodesty of being naked. Together with their knowledge of God's explicit commands to them and a sense of personal responsibility to live up to the will of their Creator, they did in fact possess a degree of blissful, natural harmony with God's will.

But without consciousness that brings with it free will, the bliss of Eden was not the ideal state of natural consciousness that Kabbalah and Chassidut speak of. The messianic state of natural consciousness, known in Kabbalah as "the construction of the persona of Rachel" (בִּנְיַן פַּרְצוּף רָחֵל), depends on the soul exercising its conscious free will to "naturally" choose good. Significantly, the numerical value of בִּנְיַן פַּרְצוּף רָחֵל (806) is equal to that of the final word of the Torah's account of creation, לַעֲשׂוֹת ("to do," in the sense of "to rectify"). The concluding phrase of the account of creation is "that God created to do." The sages interpret this seemingly redundant phrase to mean that God created the world for *us* "to do" (i.e., to complete), to bring creation to it ultimate state of rectification. It is for us to construct in full the persona of Rachel, to achieve the ideal state of "natural consciousness" for which we were created.

The number 806 is the product of the numerical values of two of God's Names, *El* = 31 and *Havayah* = 26. In Kabbalah, the Name *El* represents God's attribute of loving-kindness to all and

---

1. See p. 44.

the Name *Havayah* represents God's attribute of infinite mercy and compassion over all. By emulating the Divine attributes of loving-kindness and compassion, we reach the ideal state of "natural consciousness," thereby completing God's creation.

16

Knowledge and the Chambers of the Heart[1]

Proverbs states: "And by knowledge are the chambers filled with all precious and pleasing riches."[2] The interpretation of the word "chambers," as referring to the six emotive/instinctive domains of the soul, is supported by the statement in the *Zohar* identifying knowledge as the "key that includes six," i.e., opens the six "chambers" of the heart from loving-kindness to foundation.

The word "chamber" (חֶדֶר), as taught in Kabbalah, is an acronym for the Hebrew words for benevolence (חֶסֶד), judgment (דִין), and mercy (רַחֲמִים), which correspond to the three primary emotive attributes of the soul, loving-kindness, strength, and beauty.[3] In a wider context they represent the three vertical axes of the soul along which all six emotive/instinctive *sefirot* align themselves (victory as the branch of loving-kindness; thanksgiving as the branch of strength; and foundation as the extension of beauty).

Each one of the six chambers, the six attributes of the heart, is referred to as a *dei'ah*, literally, an opinion or a characteristic (as the term is used by Maimonides in the section of his code called *Hilchot Dei'ot*). The word *dei'ah* is a variant noun form of knowledge, *da'at*. This linguistic phenomenon beautifully illustrates our fundamental premise that knowledge is the all-inclusive *sefirah*,

---

1. See p. 49.

2. Proverbs 24:4.

3. See Rabbi Moshe Cordovero's *Pardes, Sha'ar Erchei HaKinuyim*.

and that in particular the conscious process of making a decision begins with the loving-kindness of knowledge, affinity, and concludes with the foundation of knowledge, decision.

The fact that numerically, "knowledge" (דַּעַת), 474, equals 6 times "opinion" (דֵּעָה), 79, clearly illustrates that knowledge contains in itself the potential of 6 opinions or alternatives, and as a key, opens their individual manifestations of consciousness in the heart.

Taking a closer look at the word chamber (חֶדֶר) as an acronym for loving-kindness, judgment, and mercy, we notice that whereas loving-kindness is the name of the *sefirah*, mercy is the name of beauty's internal quality; judgment in this case refers to an intermediate stage between the *sefirah* of strength and its internal aspect of awe. Thus, chamber as an acronym involves a progressive penetration from the outer expression of the *sefirah* to the inner experience/lifeforce of the *sefirah*. Indeed, the root of chamber in Hebrew, means "to penetrate!" From this we learn that the objective of knowledge is to penetrate the chambers of our hearts until we reach—experience and become motivated to implement—the attribute of mercy.

17

"If I am not for Myself…"[1]

The division of knowledge into cognitive, emotive and instinctual powers is figuratively alluded to in the three well-known queries of Hillel: "If I am not for myself, who shall be for me? Yet when I am for myself alone, what good am I? And if not now, when?"[2]

The first query—"If I am not for myself, who shall be for me?"—alludes to the self-reliance associated with the cognitive forces of knowledge (from the crown of knowledge to the knowledge of knowledge).

The second query—"Yet when I am for myself alone, what good am I?"—alludes to the emotive forces of knowledge (from the loving-kindness of knowledge to the beauty of knowledge) that negotiate interpersonal relationships.

The third and final query—"And if not now, when?"—alludes to the instinctual forces of knowledge (from victory of knowledge to foundation of knowledge), which push for an immediate resolution of uncertainty, leading to decisive action. Numerically, the three words, "and if not now" (וְאִם לֹא עַכְשָׁו) equal 474, which is also the numerical value of knowledge (דַּעַת). As we saw above, the power of knowledge comes to its forte in the instinctual forces of the soul.

---

1. See p. 59.
2. *Avot* 1:14

18

Knowledge and Possession[1]

The concepts of acquisition (*kinyan*) and consciousness/knowledge are explicitly linked in the verse: "An astute heart will acquire [*yikneh*] knowledge."[2] Elsewhere, the concept of possession appears in connection with the two other cognitive powers, wisdom and understanding.[3] The sages also connect these two terms in the *Midrash*:[4]

> If you have acquired knowledge (*da'at kanita*), what do you lack? If you are lacking knowledge, what have you acquired?

The few instances in the Bible in which the term "possession" is not applied strictly to monetary acquisition refer either to the attainment of knowledge, as in the sources quoted above, or to the possession of one's creative output—as in the phrase: "[God,] Possessor of heavens and earth."[5] Eve's use of the term fits the latter connotation: "I have possessed a man,"[6] by virtue of having formed him and given him life.

In Jewish law, the relationship between possession and knowledge is reflected in the condition, relevant to most forms of legal acquisition, that both parties be "possessed of knowledge," i.e., the requisite psychological and intellectual maturity that renders one responsible for one's actions. The act of betrothal is

---

1. See p. 69.

2. Proverbs 18:15.

3. Proverbs 4:5,7; 16:16; 17:16.

4. *Vayikra Rabbah* 1.

5. Genesis 14:19, 22; see also Deuteronomy 32:6, Proverbs 8:22 et al.

6. Genesis 4:1.

itself a form of legal acquisition, and thereby predicated upon the knowledge and consent of both parties.

19

The Primordial Origins of the Masculine and Feminine[1]

The primordial division of reality into distinct male and female aspects is referred to in Kabbalah as the bisection (*nesirah*). It represents a series of supernal maneuvers aimed at severing the initial back-to-back attachment of the adjoining male and female *partzufim* (*Ze'ir Anpin* and *Nukvei Dize'ir Anpin*) associated with the seven Divine emotive attributes that govern reality. Their subsequent face-to-face meeting and re-union is what inspires the supreme "unification" of God's own male and female aspects.

Another name in Kabbalah for this rectified state of the emotive attributes is "balance" (*matkela*, which literally means "scales"), a term that the Arizal, identifies as the balance between the forces of male and female in creation.[2] This term first appears in a key section of the *Zohar* known as the *Sifra Detzni'uta* (the Shrouded Book), which states:

> Prior to the *matkela*, they were unable to look at each other face-to-face. The primordial kings died, their crowns were not apparent, and the earth was laid to waste.

This cryptic statement is interpreted as referring to the chaotic realm (*olam hatohu*) that reigned prior to the initiation of the rectified realm (*olam hatikun*) associated with balance. The primordial kings mentioned represent the seven emotive attributes (*midot*) that governed and directed creation in the chaotic realm.

---

1. See p. 81.

2. *Sha'ar Ma'amarei Rashbi, Terumah.*

Supernally analogous to the succession of Edomite kings cited in Genesis,[3] these immature forces were fated to extinction because of their inability "to look at each other face-to-face" and thereby achieve union. This primordial defect was ultimately rooted in the unrectified conjunction of pleasure and will in the crown of these kings.

The effects of this unrectified state of conjunction on reality correspond in Kabbalah to a succession of ill-begat generations starting with pleasure and will in the crown as the "grandparents," personified in the name of the *partzufim Atik Yomin* and *Arich Anpin*. As their relationship did not mature, their immediate "offspring"—the conscious forces of wisdom and understanding, personified as the *partzufim* of *Abba* and *Ima*—were unable to face each other. Therefore, the element of strict judgment (*din*) indigenous to *Ima* was left unsweetened by the mercy (*rachamim*) that *Abba* could convey to his supernal mate only when inspired by the compassionate embrace of *Atik* and *Arich* themselves.

Consequently, their "children" (the seven emotive attributes), who were now the "third generation," were left to be "raised" by an overly severe *Ima*, while neglected by their *Abba* and deprived of the mercy that normally flows from one's loving "elders" (again, *Atik* and *Arich*). Inheriting their mother's unmitigated strict judgment, these "children," the seven emotive attributes, went on to rule reality as the seven primordial kings whose "crowns [of mercy] were not apparent." Incapable of "looking at each other face-to-face," their sterile rule led to the wasting of creation and their own eventual extinction—like the Edomite kings who died in quick succession, without wives or heirs.

It is only when *Atik* and *Arich* foresee the inherent potential of their offspring—the seven emotive attributes destined to emerge from knowledge, the mediating between the *partzufim* of *Abba* and *Ima*—that they succeed in aligning themselves to one

---

3. See Genesis 36:31ff.

another in mature, rectified balance. They then inspire *Abba* and *Ima* to face one another, allowing the mercy of the crown to be showered upon their children. The rectified dominion of the balance (*matkela*) ensues as the supernal forces governing reality, the male and female *partzufim* of *Ze'ir* and *Nukva*, are united face-to-face.

Although the balance has its origin in the alignment of *Atik* and *Arich*, it becomes fully manifest outside the crown, first in the symmetry of *Abba* and *Ima,* and then in the balance of *Ze'ir* and *Nukva* themselves. This is due to the lack of (relational) symmetry within the crown. Relational symmetry implies dichotomy but the realm of crown is too closely united with God—Who is, of course, completely and singularly One, and therefore possesses no internal dichotomies that could result in symmetry. Hence, the *Zohar* describes the crown as "entirely identified with the right, the side of mercy." However, the other *sefirot* all possess varying degrees of both "left" (the side of judgment) and "right" (the side of mercy), and thus they alone can adequately demonstrate the dynamic of balance in creation.

The instatement of balance, and its corresponding rectified realm, is alluded to in the reign of Hadar, the eighth Edomite king, whose kingship survived due to his having achieved balance through marriage to Meheitavel. The kings of Israel who reigned after him elevated creation to its highest level of rectification through their consummate harmonization of judgment and mercy.[4]

---

4. See Rashi's commentary to Genesis 1:1 s.v. "Elokim," [based on *Bereishit Rabbah* 12:15] for a parallel account of God's two operational models for creation: the initial one of judgment, which subsequently co-opted by that of mercy.

20

A Whole and a Half[1]

The depiction of woman as having developed from one "side" of man[2] reflects the principle of union between a whole and a half (*shalem va'chetzi*) taught by the early medieval Kabbalist, Rabbi Abraham Abulafia. This principle, when applied to the male-female relationship, implies, somewhat paradoxically, that the initially whole male can only find completion through the female who is referred to as his half.

This idea is supported by the Kabbalistic identification of male and female with the letters *yud* (י) and *hei* (ה), the first two letters of God's essential Name, *Havayah* (י-הוה) which themselves compose a Divine Name, י-ה. The *yud* (י) that corresponds to man equals 10 and the *hei* (ה) that corresponds to woman equals 5, thus exhibiting a ratio of one to one-half. In addition, these two letters, *yud* and *hei*, distinguish between the words for man (אִישׁ) and woman (אִשָּׁה), of which it is said: "When they merit, the Divine Presence [represented by the two letters of the Divine Name *yud-hei*] dwells between them."[3]

---

1. See p. 81.

2. See Genesis 2:22.

3. *Sotah* 17a.

21

Fraternity and Marriage[1]

One of the sources for describing the core relationship between a husband and wife as fraternal is the following verse:

> Were it that you could be as my brother, nursing at my mother's breasts; I would find you outside and kiss you, nor would anyone scorn me.[2]

"As my brother" (כְּאָח) can be seen as an acronym and a symbolic reference to the union of Adam and Chavah (whose names begin with the letter א and ח) originating in the super-conscious crown of the soul (כֶּתֶר, which begins with the letter כ of כְּאָח) where the two souls are united at their root.

This idea is also alluded to in a metaphorical image describing the creation of man: "Back and front You have fashioned me, and placed upon me Your palm."[3] In this verse Adam and Eve, the "back" and "front" of primordial man, are described as suspended beneath the hovering "palm" of God. In Hebrew the word for palm is *kaf*, the name of the letter כ. In addition, the numerical value of the letter *kaf* is equal to fraternity (אַחֲוָה), 20.

We might ask how "the beloved" learns that her relationship with her groom might be fraternal? By analyzing the text we find an answer fitting to our own discussion. Let us take a look at the original Hebrew verse:

מִי יִתֶּנְךָ כְּאָח לִי יוֹנֵק שְׁדֵי אִמִּי אֶמְצָאֲךָ בַחוּץ אֶשָּׁקְךָ גַּם לֹא יָבֻזוּ לִי

---

1. See p. 82.
2. Song of Songs 8:1.
3. Psalms 139:5.

Only those words that have an odd number of letters contain a middle letter. They are: כאח שדי אמי אמצאך Combining their middle letters we get אדמצ. The first three letters form the word Adam (אדם), while the fourth, צ, equals 90, which is twice the numerical value of *Adam* (אדם = 45). So the value of all 4 middle letters is 3 times Adam (אדם אדם אדם = 135). We may therefore say that Adam is the brother to whom the verse refers to implicitly and his relationship with his own beloved, Eve, serves as the source for this verse.

Note also that the value of the word for fraternal (כְּאָח), 29, is the difference between these four letters (אדמצ), 135 and the value of the three words *kaf Adam Chavah* (כף אדם חוה), 164, whose acronym spells כְּאָח!

22

Eternal Fraternity[1]

The nearest the Torah comes to expressing a referant for the fraternal relationship is through the word "flesh" (*she'eir*), which generally refers to immediate blood kin, but in at least one instance alludes specifically to one's wife.[2] In that reference, which appears in the priestly laws forbidding contact with a dead body, the priest is explicitly permitted to care for the body of his wife (*she'airo hakarov ailav*, "his flesh, closest to him") and other immediate kin.

The rabbinic sources[3] on this verse go as far as to say that "there is no meaning to *she'eir* other than one's wife," alluding to the profound identification between man and wife that can only be expressed in terms of "flesh-and-blood" kinship (evoking the verse: "bone of my bone, flesh of my flesh"[4]). The fraternity implicit in the relationship of *she'eir* perseveres even in face of the normally severe laws prohibiting ritual defilement, unlike the physical bond of love, which is suspended in the event of menstrual impurity.

The deep identification between husband and wife expressed in the relationship of *she'eir* is reflected in an alternate meaning of the word: a "remnant." As individual selves, man and wife are mere remnants of a primordial whole in which their souls are bound together at their root. Yet each retains the immortality

---

1. See p. 83.

2. Leviticus 21:2.

3. See *Torat Cohanim ad loc.*

4. Genesis 2:23.

(*hasharah*)—a word that stems from the same root as *she'eir*—that destines them to remain together for all eternity.

This idea is reflected in the sages' interpretation of Joseph's seduction by the wife of his master, Potiphar: "And as she spoke with Joseph each day, he did not heed her to lie beside her, to be with her."[5] According to the sages, the phrase "to lie beside her" implies "even without physical relations," whereas "to be with her," suggests their remaining together "in the World to Come."[6] If we interpret lying together without physical relations as an allusion to joint burial, then both expressions seem to suggest that the temptation was not a fleeting passion, but the desire for everlasting fraternity. This idea is given further support by the *Midrash* that identifies Osnat, Joseph's eventual wife, who was raised in Potiphar's home, as the daughter of his sister, Dinah.[7] Hence, Potiphar's wife did serve in some capacity as Joseph's surrogate sister, relating her feeling of fraternity for him.

---

5. Genesis 39:10.

6. *Sotah* 3b; *Bereishit Rabbah* 87:6

7. *Pirkei d'Rabbi Eliezer* beginning of chapter 38.

23

Fraternity and Unity[1]

According to the Medieval grammarian Rabbi David Kimchi, the Radak, in the verse: "...and he did one from one of these"[2] the word *ach* is synonymous with the word "one" (*echad*). Therefore, the Radak concludes that אח must be the two-letter sub-root of אחד from the fact that the feminine "one," אַחַת, drops the final ד of the three-letter root אחד.

Conceptually, one might consider the two-letter sub-root אח as representing oneness in the sense of absolute "singularity," whereas אחד symbolizes the function of "one" as the common divisor of every integer. This fits nicely with the interpretation in Kabbalah of the word *echad* as the combination of a male force associated with the letters *a-ch* (i.e., singularity), and a female force identified with the letter *dalet* (equal to four; i.e., the power to expand spatially in all four directions).

Another interpretation of the root אחד, which pertains to our discussion, views it as the initials of *Adam, Chavah*, and *da'at* (knowledge, the power that binds them).

Numerically, *ach* (אָח), 9, and *echad* (אֶחָד), 13, equal *yachad* (יַחַד), 22, which means together. In Kabbalah, one of the classifications of the 22 letters of the Hebrew alphabet divides them into 9 and 13 letters.[3] When 22 is multiplied by 19, the numerical value of *Chavah*, the first woman, the result is 418, the combined value of *ach*, 9, and *achat* (אַחַת, the feminine "one"), 409.

---

1. See p. 83.

2. Ezekiel 18:10. The original Hebrew reads: וְעָשָׂה אָח מֵאַחַד מֵאֵלֶּה.

3. See *Teshuvat Hashanah*, pp. 82-3.

24

Fraternity and Love[1]

The clearest Biblical reference to the fraternity implicit in one's relationship to one's spouse appears in the similar accounts of Abraham and Isaac's experiences dwelling among heathens. Fearful that the heathen might kill them for their wives, both men referred to their wives as their "sisters."[2] In the case of Abraham, his wife Sarah *was* to an extent his sister,[3] insofar as she was his niece, born to his brother Haran. In the case of Isaac, Rebecca was his cousin.

The foremost indication of the place of fraternity within marriage lies in the rabbinic endorsement of marrying one's niece; in particular, the daughter of one's sister (as in the case of Joseph and his niece, Osnat), so that one's natural affection for one's sister (who one is forbidden to marry) extend to one's wife. This is alluded to by the expression: "...and from your flesh, do not hide yourself,"[4] suggesting that fraternity within a relationship reduces the degree to which the partners conceal themselves from each other.

Elsewhere in Jewish tradition, one is exhorted before choosing a wife to investigate his prospective brother-in-law.[5] So was the case of Aaron, who saw in his bride, Elisheva, the noble qualities of her brother Nachshon, the prince of Judah. While the

---

1. See p. 83.
2. Genesis 12:13 and 26:7, respectively.
3. See Ibid. 20:12.
4. Isaiah 58:7.
5. *Baba Batra* 110a.

reason for this is the expectation that one's children will inherit facets of the brother-in-law's character, it can also be said that admiration and identification with one's brother-in-law will foster fraternity within one's marriage itself.

The Hebrew words for "fraternity" (אַחֲוָה) and "love" (אַהֲבָה) possess four letters each. Multiplying each letter of אחוה with the corresponding letter of אהבה and taking the sum we get 78 (א · א = 1; ה · ה = 40; ו · ב = 12; ה · ה = 25). 78 equals 6 times 13 where 13 is the numerical value of both "love" (אַהֲבָה) and "one" (אֶחָד).

In Kabbalah, the full set of permutations of a word's letters is considered its ultimate extension. The three letters of "one" can be permutated 6 different ways. The total value of all six permutations is 78, the number that results from the "multiplication" of the Hebrew words for fraternity and love, or in other words, the super-conscious source of love and its conscious revelation.

25

Image and Likeness[1]

The primacy of "image" (*tzelem*) over "likeness" (*demut*) can be inferred from their order in the verse: "And God said: Let us make man in our image, similar to our likeness;"[2] first "image," then "likeness." In addition, grammatically, "image" appears with the preposition "in," indicating that it was applied precisely to man's form, but the word "likeness" appears with the imprecise modifier "similar to." Hence, image implies a more immediate identification with God than that indicated by likeness.

Another indication of the image's primacy in man's creation is that sequentially multiplying the letters of the word for Adam (א times ד times מ) yields the same value as that of "image" (צֶלֶם), 160. Furthermore, the composition of the name *Adam* (אדם) itself alludes to the combination of image—represented by the *alef* (א), its first letter, symbolic of God's absolute unity—and likeness, whose two-letter sub-root, דם, account for the remaining letters.

Interestingly enough, the order of image and likeness is inverted in the verse describing the birth of Adam's son, Seth: "And he [Adam] begat a child in his likeness and according to his image."[3] Not only do the two words switch positions, but they even exchange prefixes, from which we learn that, as though physically we resemble our parents, our soul mirrors the "image" of God more perfectly than it does the image of our own father. We can only approximate the "image" of our fathers ("*according* to

---

1. See p. 84.
2. Genesis 1:26.
3. Ibid. 5:3.

his image"), but cannot replicate it. Nevertheless, in emulating the *ways* of our fathers, we achieve a more perfect likeness ("in his likeness") than we do when emulating the ways of God.

26

Silent Speech[1]

The verse: "To You, silence is praise, O God in Zion"[2] links silence (*dumiyah*) with speech. The praise in this verse refers to the silent song of the soul that fills super-consciousness with praise of God, the Creator. The verse suggests that the union of silence and praise/speech in the soul brings about a corresponding union between God and Zion, symbolizing the revelation of God's kingship in the material realm.

This identification of silence with speech recalls the practice of the "early pietists" who, in preparation for prayer, would "linger for an hour" in silent meditation, thereby hoping to infuse their praise of God with the spirit of silence.[3]

The idea that silence and speech coexist as a single force is referred to in Kabbalistic and Chassidic sources as the oscillation of the *chashmal*, a term borrowed from Ezekiel's vision of the heavenly chariot.[4] As such, *chashmal* represents the Divine synergy of silence (*chash*) and speech (*mal*)—the effect of God's oscillation between revelation and concealment within the created order.

The numerical union of sound, or voice (קוֹל = 136) and silence (דְּמָמָה = 89) as in the idiom "the sound of subtle silence" (*kol demamah dakah*), is 225 or 15^2, the value of choice (בְּחִירָה). It is the sound within the inner silence of our soul's super-consciousness, as it speaks to God while resonating with the

---

1. See p. 87.
2. Psalms 65:2.
3. See *Berachot* 30b.
4. See Ezekiel 1:27.

vibrations it receives from outer reality that is the origin of our power to choose.

27

The Living-Uttering Spirit[1]

The speech of super-consciousness is analogous to the root of Eve within the soul of Adam. The name Eve (*Chavah*) connotes expression and more specifically suggests the expression of speech. This is evident from Onkolos, who translates the expression "a living spirit"[2] (*nefesh chayah*) as "an uttering spirit" (*ruach memalela*). The word for spirit here, *chayah*, is the same as Eve's "ideal" name.[3] This "living spirit," which is identified in the verse with newly-created man, represents the primordial root of Eve within the soul of Adam.

The average value of *nefesh chayah* (נֶפֶשׁ חַיָּה = 453), *ish ishah* (אִישׁ אִשָּׁה = 617), and *Adam Chavah* (אָדָם חַוָּה = 64) is equal to the value of *chashmal* (חַשְׁמַל = 378), the mysterious word of Ezekiel that unifies the silence of man (*chash*) with the speech of woman (*mal*), as explained above.

Living soul (*nefesh chayah*) reflects the super-conscious root of the union of man and woman and corresponds to the upper tip of the *yud* of the Name *Havayah*.

Man-woman reflects the couple's union in higher consciousness and corresponds to the higher union of the *yud* and the first *hei* of *Havayah*, the *yud* of אִישׁ and the *hei* of אִשָּׁה.

Finally, Adam-Eve, their given names, reflect union in the lower consciousness and correspond to the lower union of the *vav* and the second *hei* of *Havayah*.

---

1. See p. 87.

2. Genesis 2:7.

3. See Rashi to Genesis 3:20. See also chapter 4, endnote 30.

	pair	union in
י upper tip of *yud*	living-soul *nefesh chayah*	super-consciousness
יה *yud hei*	man-woman *ish-ishah*	higher consciousness
וה *vav hei*	Adam-Eve	lower consciousness

28

The Redemptive Power of Love[1]

The name of the tractate in which the *Mishnah* describing the courtship ritual appears is *Ta'anit*, which literally means "fast," as the general topic of the tractate is the laws of fast days. That this *mishnah* appears at the conclusion of this tractate hints at the beneficial effect that fasting has on one's capacity to decide with regard to marriage. It is, in fact, a common custom for the bride and groom to fast on their wedding day. Purging themselves physically prepares them to conclude their commitments with proper spiritual clarity.

The numerical value of the word for fast (תַּעֲנִית) is 930, the same number as the years of the life of Adam.[2] Of those years, 130 (= עני, the root letters of תַּעֲנִית) were spent in voluntary abstention from marital relations, in repentance for the primordial sin, prior to resuming that sacred commitment for the remaining 800 (= תת, the prefix and suffix letters of תַּעֲנִית) years of his life.

The obvious reason for including the account of the dancing maidens in this tractate lies in its identification of days associated with fasting (Yom Kippur and the 15th of *Av*, following *Tisha Be'av*, the 9th of Av, the fast commemorating the destruction of the first and second Temples) as the appropriate times for staging this rite of courtship. These two days represent the high points of *Av* and *Tishrei*—months that are especially suited to making love-related choices.

---

1. See p. 91.
2. Genesis 5:5.

The word *Av*, related to the root *avah* ("desire"), is also the two-letter sub-root of the word *ahavah* ("love"), indicating the appropriateness of the month as a time for seeking the object of one's heart's desire. The bitter association of *Av* with the destruction of the Temple and the concomitant loss of the revelation of God's Presence provides a poignantly meaningful backdrop to the pursuit of restored wholeness through marriage.

Whereas the ritual in *Av* affords the opportunity to discern the inner direction of one's desire, the articulation of that discovery may come only after the rite is repeated two months later, on Yom Kippur. That special day, commemorating God's reaffirmed commitment to Israel through forgiveness and conciliation, is uniquely suited as a day for affirming other inspired commitments.

Together, the 15th of *Av* and Yom Kippur highlight the redemptive power of love, enabling one to rebuild one's life on new foundations. This is reinforced by the allusion to the first word of the Torah, *bereishit* (בְּרֵאשִׁית) which means "in the beginning," whose six letters comprise the two words *Av* (אָב) and *Tishrei* (תִּשְׁרֵי).

29

Simple, Double, Triple, and Quadruple Song[1]

The account of the rite of the dancing maidens appearing in the Jerusalem Talmud[2] differs from the description appearing in the Babylonian Talmud. The Jerusalem Talmud, having been compiled earlier than its Babylonian counterpart, more closely reflects the style and language of the *Mishnah*. According to Kabbalah, the condensed language of the Jerusalem Talmud derives from its source in abstract wisdom, whereas the more elaborate expositions typical of the Babylonian Talmud stem from its association with understanding.

Thus, the Jerusalem Talmud speaks of only two pleas: "The unattractive ones would say: Do not set your eyes upon beauty. The pretty ones would say: Set your eyes on family." In contrast to the *Gemara* of the Babylonian Talmud, which introduces entreaties not found in the *Mishnah*, this account conserves the *Mishnah*'s version of the plea ("Do not set your eyes upon beauty; set your eyes upon family!") while attributing its component clauses to two different classes of maiden.

One might suggest, as well, that the "pretty ones" referred to in the Jerusalem Talmud include the three attractive types (the pretty, the pedigreed, and the wealthy) alluded to in the Babylonian version. This would in effect modify the implication that the only distinction significant to the Jerusalem Talmud was physical

---

1. See p. 92.

2. *Ta'anit* 4:7.

183

beauty. This approach, put forth by the Lubavitcher Rebbe,[3] implies that the "family" advantage promoted by the "pretty ones" encompasses all manner of inherited privilege—be it beauty, wealth, or breeding. Whereas in the Babylonian version these three ranks proudly single themselves out, in the *Jerusalem Talmud* they band together in humble acknowledgment of the fact that their respective assets come by inheritance rather than through any merit of their own.

The "unattractive ones" referred to in the *Jerusalem Talmud* express an even more humble attitude. Believing that true virtue derives from the Divine spark within, these young maidens urge one to ignore outer appearances altogether, and focus instead upon Divine Providence: The language of the *Mishnah* supports this contention. There, the maidens preface their plea with the words, "Young man, lift up your eyes and see"—words that evoke the verse: "Lift your eyes heavenward and see..."[4] the hand of Divine Providence.

The elaboration of the *Mishnah* through its interpretation and elaboration in the Jerusalem and Babylonian Talmuds reflects an interesting numerical progression, whereby the single group of women referred to in the *Mishnah* divides into four separate groups:

• The *Mishnah*: the "daughters of Jerusalem"

• The Jerusalem Talmud: the "unattractive ones" and the "pretty ones"

• The Babylonian Talmud: the "pretty ones" and the "pedigreed ones" and the "unattractive ones"

• The *Ein Yaakov*'s version: the "pretty ones" and the "pedigreed ones" and the "wealthy ones" and the "unattractive ones"

---

3. *Likutei Sichot*, Vol. 19, p. 80.

4. Isaiah 40:26.

This progression corresponds to the supernal evolution of rhythm in song, as described in Kabbalah.[5] The relationship between the rhythm of song and dance serves to elaborate on the correlation:

The simple song (*shir pashut*), or 1/4 time: possessed of an open and free rhythm, this "song" can be said to have no tempo at all. Hence, it corresponds to the *Mishnah*, which resists any differentiation whatsoever between component classes of maiden, thereby leaving their rhythmic interplay undefined.

The dual song (*shir kaful*), or 2/4 time: based upon the elementary up and down beats, this is the core of all rhythmic construction. It corresponds to the classification of the *Jerusalem Talmud*, which offers a basic division between the "pretty" (upbeat) and the "unattractive" (downbeat).

The triple song (*shir meshulash*), or 3/4 time: this first extension of beat into a mature rhythmic progression, while lacking full balance, is the primary basis for the composition of song. It corresponds to the classification of the Babylonian Talmud—the first that provides a more or less complete three-part articulation of the interacting personalities among the "daughters of Jerusalem."

The quadruple song (*shir meruba*), or 4/4 time: a fully balanced rhythmic construction, allowing optimal musical expression, it corresponds to the classification of the *Ein Yaakov*, completing the *Gemara*'s expansion of the *Mishnah*'s unit into four separate groupings.

---

5. *Zohar* III:219b.

30

Virtue, Pleasure, and Profit[1]

Together, the initial letters of virtue (טוֹב), pleasure (עָרֵב) and profit (מוֹעִיל) spell the Hebrew word meaning "reason," or "taste" (טעם), as in a tasteful or palatable reason for choosing.

The tripartite division of the Maharsha parallels the Kabbalistic classification of the nine conscious *sefirot*, from wisdom to foundation, into three general groupings, each including three *sefirot*, one to the right, one to the left, and one to the middle: the intellectual (*muskal*) *sefirot* are wisdom, understanding, and knowledge; the emotional (*murgash*) *sefirot* are loving-kindness, strength, and beauty; and the instinctual (*mutba*) *sefirot* are victory, thanksgiving, and foundation. The intellectual powers of the soul seek virtue; the emotive forces seek pleasure; while the instinctive traits are aimed at expediency.

As is explained in the text, the origin of these three classes is in the super-consciousness of the soul, the three "heads" of the *sefirah* of crown. The origin of virtue is in the soul's super-conscious power of faith, "the unknowable head" (*radla*) of the crown. The origin of pleasure is in the soul's super-conscious experience of pleasure, "the head of nothingness" (*reisha d'ayin*) of the crown. The origin of expedience is in the soul's super-conscious drive of will, "the long, patient head" (*reisha d'arich*) of the crown.

Indeed, the average value of these three pairs of words in Hebrew: virtue/faith (טוֹב אֱמוּנָה = 119), pleasure/pleasure (תַּעֲנוּג עָרֵב = 801) and expedient/will (מוֹעִיל רָצוֹן = 502) is equal to the

---

1. See p. 93.

186

value of the word for knowledge, or choice (דַעַת = 474), the seat of the soul's power of choice! For more on the conceptual and numerical relationship between faith and virtue (or good).[2]

At the conscious level of the soul, the essential state of consciousness of each of the three classes described above is that of the *sefirah* that lies on its middle, balancing axis:

- Virtue is essentially a consciousness of the *sefirah* of knowledge whose corresponding Divine Name in Kabbalah is אהוה (= 17), which numerically equals virtue (טוֹב); and, whose archetypal soul, Moses, was first named, by his mother *tov*.[3]

- Pleasure is the consciousness exhibited by the *sefirah* of beauty whose archetypal soul, Jacob, was attracted to his wife Rachel by her beauty. In Hebrew this specific word for pleasureable (*arev*) connotes a mixture or blend of different tastes, just as beauty implies a blend of different colors.

- Finally, expedience or profit are the types of consciousness expressed by the *sefirah* of foundation whose archetypal soul, Joseph—described as the "successful man"[4]—is numerically equivalent to "expedience" (מוֹעִיל = יוֹסֵף = 156).

The average numerical value of these three pairs of motivator and archetypal soul: Moses/virtue (טוֹב מֹשֶׁה = 362), Jacob/pleasure (עָרֵב יַעֲקֹב = 454), and Joseph/expedience (יוֹסֵף מוֹעִיל = 312) is equal to 376 the value of *shalom* (שָׁלוֹם), the

---

2. See chapter 1, endnote 18.

3. *Sotah* 12a.

4. Genesis 39:2.

Hebrew word for "peace," which is ultimately the ideal objective in choosing a partner for marriage!

31

Clarification by Direct and Reflected Light[1]

The combined force of direct light and reflected light is symbolized in the shape of the Hebrew letter *chet* (ח) which is graphically constructed from a *vav* (ו) and a *zayin* (ז). The letter *vav* is used in Hebrew as a conjunctive "and," therefore symbolizing the clarity of direct light descending to connect the individual with reality. The *zayin*, which graphically has a crown that represents the primordial root to which it ascends, symbolizes the clarity of the reflected light.

These two letters are also associated in Kabbalah with the male and female: the *vav* (whose numerical value is 6) alludes to the six *sefirot* of active male influence (from loving-kindness to foundation), while the *zayin* (numerical value 7) represents the seventh *sefirah*, kingdom, the feminine receptive force within creation that follows them.

In addition, the crown upon the *zayin* evokes the verse: "A woman of valor is the crown of her husband."[2] The small upper bridge that unites these two letters into the letter *chet* can be thought of as the bridal canopy hovering above the male and female forces of clarity.

We can now interpret the grammatical root of choice, בחר, as an allusion to the central role that consciousness plays in the clarification of reality. The root's outer letters, *bet* and *reish*, taken

---

1. See p. 110.
2. Proverbs 12:14.

together are the two-letter sub-root of "clarification," while the *chet*, the letter that appears in the center, symbolizes the direct and reflected light of consciousness, as above.

Endnotes

Preface

1. *Tanya*, ibid., end of chapter 1.

2. See also *Sod Hashem Liyereiav*, chapter 8.

3. *Tanya, Sha'ar Hayichud Veha'emuna*, chapter 7, based on Maimonides' statement that "He is the Knower, He is the Known and He is Knowledge itself."

4. Maimonides' statement in endnote 3.

5. Genesis 2:19.

6. See *Tanya*, ibid., chapter 1.

7. *Bereishit Rabbah* 17:4.

8. Although Adam possessed the level of consciousness necessary to call things by name, before eating the forbidden fruit of the Tree of Knowledge of Good and Evil, he and Eve were unable to distinguish between the polarities of good and evil (Rashi to Genesis ibid.). Only after the primordial sin did man's consciousness begin to function in accordance with the binary, value-oriented logic of good versus evil and right versus wrong.

9. In Chassidic thought (see the Tzemach Tzedek's *Derech Mitzvotecha, Mitzvat Priya U'reviya*), it is explained that the ability to procreate, to give birth to offspring, is the human exemplar of the same type of infinite power (infinite both in scope and in deed) attributed to the Creator.

10. Even when physical procreation is not possible, be it for temporary or permanent reasons, the marital bond between husband and wife always entails spiritual procreation, augmenting the revealed presence of God in the world.

11. Genesis 1:28. *Tur, Even Haezer* 1.

12. The *Ba'al Shem Tov* is the popular name of Rabbi Israel ben Eliezer (1698-1760), founder of the Chassidic movement. *Ba'al Shem Tov* means "Master of the Good Name [of God]."

Introduction

1. See "Consciousness and Knowledge" (p. 127).

2. See *Sod Hashem Liyereiav*, pp. 30ff.

3. Amos 3:2.

4. Ibid., *Targum Yonatan* and *Radak*.

5. Rabbi Hillel of Paritch, a 19th century Chassidic master, in his commentary on Rabbi Dov Ber Schneersohn's *Sha'ar Ha'yichud*, explains how this process functions:

> Knowledge is a compression of thought, whereby one collects all the power of his thought and intellect so as to concentrate exclusively on one particular idea. As is known, wherever a man's thoughts are directed, that is where his entire being is invested. Hence, through knowledge one connects the entire essence of one's soul to the idea being considered....
>
> Knowledge is not the intellect nor the understanding, but rather the self-attachment alone. This can be understood by imagining two men, both of equal intelligence. One attaches himself to an idea so single-mindedly that he forgets himself entirely, while the other may not be attached at all, and instead finds himself distracted by other thoughts. Hence, the latter finds himself incapable of dwelling on the idea, while the

former can concentrate on it indefinitely... This is the power of knowledge....

6. See "Functional Levels of Knowledge" (p. 130).

7. In Kabbalah, these powers of intellect are known as the *sefirot* of wisdom and understanding. They are also referred to symbolically as the father and mother of consciousness within the soul, for together they give birth to the emotive attributes of the soul, which are referred to as the children of consciousness. Knowledge is here the power that unites the soul's father and mother principles, as in the verse, "And Adam knew [*yada*, the verb form of knowledge] his wife Eve, and she became pregnant and gave birth to Cain..." (Genesis 4:1). See *Tanya* chapter 3 and *Igeret Hakodesh* (epistle) 15.

8. Higher consciousness (*da'at elyon*) is also known as hidden consciousness (*da'at hane'elam*), for it serves to unite the soul's two concealed levels, wisdom and understanding [based on the introduction to *Tikunei Zohar*'s statement: "wisdom... and understanding..., of these two it is said 'the concealed things are to *Havayah*, our God' (Deuteronomy 29:28)]." In so doing, higher consciousness' presence in affecting the union remains invisible (for in the Kabbalistic framework father and mother never separate, negating the possibility of ever witnessing the act of their union), thereby lacking any degree of self-consciousness. For this reason, those souls that achieve this level of consciousness—as did Moses in full—feel no sense of self-accomplishment and naturally attribute all of their success to God.

9. This level of intellect is known in Chassidic thought as pure intellect (*mochin be'etzem*), in contrast to the level of intellect that relates and gives rise to the emotive attributes of the soul, intellect related to emotion (*mochin hashayachim lamidot*).

10. Higher consciousness can only be attained after the conflict between "good" and "evil"—which injects a constant fog

into our awareness—has been resolved. Higher consciousness sees reality as essentially good, for God, the Creator and ultimate essence of all reality, is the absolute good (*tov be'etzem*). No sense of "evil" can reside in a world whose consciousness is exclusively that of the presence of God. See Psalms 5:5. See also "Clarifying Reality," p. 40ff.

11. Higher consciousness (*da'at elyon*) is depicted in Chassidic thought as self illuminating light (*or hame'ir le'atzmo*) and lower consciousness (*da'at tachton*) as light illuminating the other (*or hame'ir lezulato*).

The initial letters of both terms are אֹהֶל, meaning tent, alluding to Jacob's tents of study (Genesis 25:27). Rashi explains that these tents were the academies of the two scholars Shem (son of Noah) and Eiver (great-grandson of Shem). Insofar as one's name expresses his essence, by meditating on the names of these two scholars we can ascertain the difference between their schools of thought.

Shem means "name," thus his academy symbolizes the self-enlightenment that comes with higher consciousness. *Eiver* means transmission (*ha'avarah*), hence his academy symbolizes the transmission (of light) from self to other—a process characteristic of lower consciousness.

In Hebrew the plural form of tent (אֹהָלִים) permutes to spell the Name of God, *Elohim* used in reference to the Divine soul of man. In Psalms (82:6) God expresses His desire in creating man that man become as *Elohim*. We may now understand this to mean that the intention of the Creator was that man possess a perfect state of consciousness as reflected in the union of husband and wife (see also "Tree of Life vs. Tree of Knowledge," p. 43ff.).

12. Lower consciousness is also known as extending consciousness (*da'at hamitpashet*), as it extends from the mind to the heart, drawing light from the mind to inspire the emotive

attributes of the heart to motivate positive interaction with one's surroundings.

13. Proverbs 19:2.

14. In Isaiah 41:7 "good" is used to describe "glue." An agent that binds two objects together is good. And so, knowledge, the unifying power of the soul is the essential good.

15. Psalms 119:66.

16. Deuteronomy 28:47.

17. As King David instructed his son Solomon (I Chronicles 28:9): "Know the God of your father and serve Him with a perfect heart and a desirous soul."

18. See "Between Intellect and Heart" (p.132).

19. In Kabbalistic sources (*Zohar* II:177a) this metaphor is called the sixfold key (*maftecha de'kalil sheet*). See the Tzemach Tzedek's *Derech Mitzvothecha*, 46a. Also see *Muda'oot Tiv'it* (*Natural Consciousness*) pp. 43-9.

20. Proverbs 24:4.

21. Because this word is so central in the framework of Kabbalistic thought, we will normally refer to it as *partzuf*—its Hebrew name. Linguistically, the word itself originates from ancient Greek and literally means "persona."

22. The usual analysis of a *partzuf* into its constituent *sefirot* reveals ten, with the most dynamic and ever-changing *sefirah*, knowledge, remaining implicit. At times, like in our own discussion of the *partzuf* of knowledge itself, knowledge must be included explicitly, giving us a *partzuf* that includes eleven *sefirot*.

Each of the constituent *sefirot* of the *partzuf* of knowledge can in-turn be analyzed as a complete *partzuf*—containing sub-elements corresponding to each of the other *sefirot*.

Chapter 1

1. The immature nature of this proto-consciousness is the subject of the verse: "for the inclination of man's heart is evil [i.e., unrectified] from his youth" (Genesis 8:21); "his youth" is explained by our sages (*Bereishit Rabbah* 34:10 and *Yerushalmi Berachot* 3:5) to refer to the moment of birth (see also Rashi *Ibid.*).

2. Among the signs of maturity that the Torah requires before granting full moral and legal responsibility to an adolescent is the appearance of pubic hair. According to Chassidic thought, hair represents the human capacity for external attachment.

The grammatical similarity of the Hebrew word for hair (שֵׂעָר) to the word meaning measure (שֵׁעַר) implies the need to properly measure the character of the other, together with the measurement of one's self in relation to the other, before attempting attachment. The hairs of puberty thus signify the capacity to measure outer and inner reality before committing oneself to a relationship.

3. This is one reason that the *sefirot* of crown (which corresponds to super-consciousness) and knowledge (which corresponds to consciousness) are generally not listed together in schemata of the ten *sefirot*. When one is conceptually manifest, the other is "hidden" (i.e., implicit). See also "Between Intellect and Heart" (p. 132), and endnote 22 to the Introduction.

A way of illustrating this relationship numerically is to consider the numerical equivalence between the Hebrew word for crown (כֶּתֶר) and the idiom for "true intent" (סוֹף דַּעַת), 620. This phrase can be interpreted as an allusion to the ultimate objective of consciousness: to verify the vision of super-consciousness in consciousness. The word *sof* (meaning "end," or "extreme") is related to *saf* ("threshold"), thus reinforcing the identification of super-consciousness as the "threshold" of consciousness.

4. See "Self and Other" (p. 135).

5. See chart on p. 7.

6. Rabbi Hillel of Paritch explains in his commentary on R. Dov Ber Schneerson's *Sha'ar HaYichud*:

> A child, though capable of attaching his consciousness to something, will easily be distracted to its opposite; unlike an adult, who is not so easily distracted, given that he is bound in the "depth of consciousness" to the thing that he desires to know. This "depth of consciousness" is synonymous with the power of "self-nullification" that resides in the third (posterior) brain, the brain of consciousness. It is through this power that one arrives at the absolute essence of something; (the power of intellect, on the other hand, called "wisdom" merely apprehends an extension of a thing's essence). And it is through this [power of "self-nullification"] that one affects a proper and deep rooting of his soul in the essence of the thing that he desires to know. As a result of this, one arouses the "edifying power" (*koach hamaskil*) to illuminate and apprehend...

This idea is also alluded to in the seminal work of *Chabad*, the *Tanya* (chapter 42).

7. When reciting the *Shema*—"Hear O Israel, GOD is our God, GOD is one" (Deuteronomy 6:4)—the affirmation of our faith in the absolute unity and omnipresence of God, we cover our eyes, for in this world (known as the "the world of deceit") our sensory impression of reality hides from us the ultimate truth that "GOD is one." Similarly, in order to commune with our soul-essence we must shut our eyes to the distractions of outer reality as we experience it at present.

8. In the terminology of the *Zohar* (II:116b, III:280b), "the inner eye of the heart," where God's "face" (i.e., transcendence,

the ultimate source of His Providence over all) is visible (see also R. Hillel of Paritch, *Commentary on Sha'ar Hayichud.*, section 3 [169a]).

9. See "Before Being Human" (p. 137).

10. The image of white-light or whiteness (*loven* in Hebrew) is particularly appropriate in representing the blinding amalgam of possibilities identified with crown. In Kabbalah, the crown is called the "supernal whiteness" (*loven ha'elyon*). It is also referred to as *levanon* (literally, "miniature whiteness"; note also that the geographic region known as Lebanon sits like a "crown" atop the Land of Israel). The Biblical figure of Lavan (literally, the "white one"), Jacob's father-in-law, can be said to represent the threatening, crown-like realm of infinite possibility that Jacob had to traverse before arriving at the knowledge-like rootedness of marriage and family.

11. As will be explained, pleasure and will represent the adjoining "male" and "female" components of crown; the Adam and Eve of super-consciousness. Adam and Eve were at first created together, joined back-to-back (*Talmud Berachot* 61a). Adam faced upwards toward the source of his soul, while Eve faced downward toward outer reality. Thus, in their initial state of being, Adam represents the psychological state of being-in-oneself, while Eve represents the state of being-in-the-world.

Subsequently, in their rectified state of facing one another, Adam retains his sense of pleasure in being-in-oneself by seeing his soul-root reflected in his wife, while Eve retains her sense of will in being-in-the-world by longing to actualize the Divine purpose of creation by uniting with her husband and bringing souls into this world.

12. These correspond to, but are not the same as, the seven lower *sefirot*, from loving-kindness through kingdom.

13. These are the inner psychological manifestations of the seven *sefirot* from loving-kindness to kingdom.

14. See "The Seven Inner Senses" (p. 139).

15. This longing of the soul is called desire (*chefetz*) in Kabbalah. The uniting of pleasure and will produces a secondary state of pleasure in the soul that accommodates the inherent complexity of outer experience. Termed compound pleasure (*ta'anug murkav*), as opposed to the elemental pleasure (*ta'anug pashut*) left untouched by will, this state is derived from the super-conscious identification of a diverse created order, sensed by the soul even as it is enwrapped within the solitary realm of crown.

16. Hence, will exemplifies the female ability to incorporate abstract essence ("seed") and fashion from it a living representation of God's creative will.

17. In the context of pleasure and will, it results in the abstract male pleasure acknowledging its need to be made concrete through will, while the executive force of feminine will admits its need for the values and ideals rooted within pleasure.

The mutual shift of orientation that leads to the "marriage" of pleasure and will is alluded to in the roots of the words for groom (*chatan*) and bride (*kalah*). The word *chatan* relates to the word *nachat*, which means "to descend," suggesting the groom's wish to descend from pleasure's natural state of free-floating abstraction into a grounding of self. *Kalah* (which derives from the word meaning "consummation") suggests the bride's consummate desire to escape the weightiness of daily reality by rising to a higher state of spirituality. This inversion in preparation for matrimony is reflected in the word for marriage, *nisuin*, linguistically alluding to the *nesiat hafachim*, or sustained paradox evident in each spouse alone upon entering marriage, and in both together as the symbiotic unit created by it.

18. In Kabbalah, the concepts faith and virtue, or good, are closely related. The numerical value of the Hebrew word for "faith" (אֱמוּנָה) is 102 ,which equals 6 times 17, the numerical value of virtue or good (טוֹב). The 6 here represents the six possible permutations of good (טוֹב).

Put another way, faith is the consummate expression of good or the ability of the soul to perceive good in every possible form, to believe that all derives from the ultimate good of God and that all is for the ultimate good of each and every one of God's creations.

19. The initial letters of these three Hebrew words: "virtuous" (טוֹב), "pleasurable" (עָרֵב) and "profitable" (מוֹעִיל) spell the word טַעַם, meaning "taste," or "reason."

Chapter 2

1. Psalms 110:10.

2. Indeed, the Hebrew word for expansion (הַרְחָבָה) is numerically equal to the word for deepening (הַעֲמָקָה), both equaling 220. [In Kabbalah, 220 represents the secret of the 10 *sefirot* multiplied by (i.e., inter-included in each of) the 22 letters of the Hebrew alphabet. When 10 and 22 are added together they yield 32, the 32 pathways of wisdom (*netivot chochmah*) with which God created the world, as related in the beginning of *Sefer Yetzirah*.] Thus, expansion of consciousness (הַרְחָבַת הָדַּעַת) also exactly equals deepening of consciousness (הַעֲמָקַת הָדַּעַת), or 1094.

3. In their relationship to consciousness, the *sefirot* of crown and wisdom are identified with the concepts of depth and breadth,

and the *sefirah* of understanding is identified with length. Rabbi Hillel of Paritch explains this in his commentary on *Sha'ar Hayichud*. In particular, Rabbi Hillel defines depth as the power to nullify one's consciousness so as to connect with the super-conscious root of an idea; he defines breadth as the ability to tolerate, in consciousness, the existence of thousands of ideas, also dependent upon self-nullification; and, finally, he defines length as the power to identify the "multiplicity of media" that give expression to a particular idea. The concept of length, in this sense, implies the forward extension of consciousness as it leaves the stationary posture of breadth and asserts itself in reality.

4. See also *Awakening the Spark Within*, pp. 34-6.

5. Numbers 27:16.

6. Ibid. 27:18.

7. For analogy's sake, one might say that Moses embodied the collective deepening of consciousness (*ha'amakat hada'at*) of the fledgling nation as it traveled through the wilderness of super-consciousness. His floating as an infant on the waters of the Nile suggests that the natural state of his soul was one of submersion in the super-conscious depths, as does the Torah's characterization of him as one "slow of speech and tongue," who found it hard to communicate the richness of his inner experience. His subsequent attainment of expansion of consciousness (*harchavat hada'at*) is alluded to by the reeds that surrounded him in the Nile, the reed expressing flexibility, yet deep rootedness.

8. Exodus 3:8. See also "The Land of Israel" (p. 141).

9. Rectified "consciousness," in general, is linked in the Bible to "good": "Without knowledge [consciousness] the soul is not good" (Proverbs 19:2).

10. Amazingly, the combined numerical value of their full names, Joshua the son of Nun (יְהוֹשֻׁעַ בִּן נוּן) 549, and Rachav the prostitute (רָחָב הַזּוֹנָה) as she is called in the Bible) Joshua 6:17;

6:25), 283, exactly equals the numerical value of the Land of Israel (אֶרֶץ יִשְׂרָאֵל), 832.

11. This expression—the light that sustains all worlds (*or hasovel kol almin*)—was originally applied in *Sefer Habahir* 102 (folio 44) to the righteous ones (*tzadikim*) who sustain the world.

12. In fact, the point of the impression is often referred to as the point of wisdom.

13. This ray of light is called the light that fills all worlds (*or ha'memalei kol almin*).

14. The expectation that creation will ultimately make this paradox manifest, thus bringing glory and sanctification to God's Name, is reflected in the root of the word ray (קַו) itself, which also serves as the two-letter root of hope (תִּקְוָה).

15. See Isaiah 11:9, 52:8, et al. The paradoxical revelation of God's Infinite Being residing within finite creation at the end of days will provide the ultimate expression of God's absolute essence. All logical paradoxes emanate from this essence, insofar as it defies rational categorization.

The ray's search for congruity in the relationship between inner and outer reality is alluded to by the verse: "Justice, justice, pursue" (Deuteronomy 16:20). Here, "pursue" can also mean "equate" (as in the term *shem nirdaf*, or "synonym"). Hence the verse can be interpreted to reflect the hope (see endnote 14) that the Divine justice at the core of reality will be revealed. The ray itself pursues that end by leaving God's Infinite Light and radiating into every layer of material reality, hoping to facilitate the reflection of creation's Divine essence.

16. Exodus 34:6.

17. See "Tolerance and Patience" (p. 143).

18. God's patience is not without end, and if humanity has not succeeded in restoring the Divine image of creation by some

affixed time, God in His mysterious wisdom will see to it that humanity fulfills its messianic potential.

19. In the words of our sages, "Just as their faces are not similar, so are their characters [*dei'oteihem*, from *da'at*, consciousness] not similar" (see *Berachot* 58a).

20. Whereas expansion was metaphorically described as a panoramic vision of created being, stability is described in terms of harmonic balance, thus reflecting Kabbalah's association of wisdom and understanding with the senses of sight and sound.

21. Of course, in the case of choosing a soulmate, this does not yet mean that we are destined to marry, just that we possess a definite spiritual affinity to one another. Each soul possesses many "relatives," though not every relative is meant to be one's spouse.

22. In Kabbalah, the three words of the Divine Name that God revealed to Moses before the Exodus, "I shall be that I shall be" (*Eheyeh asher Eheyeh*), are seen to correspond to the first three *sefirot*, crown, wisdom and understanding. Thus, the word that appears first and last, "I shall be," corresponds to the *sefirot* of crown and understanding, while the second word, "that"— implying the power of transition from the first "I shall be" to the second—corresponds to the *sefirah* of wisdom. The last "I shall be" expresses a definite kind of anchoring force on the self. The first "I shall be" (of crown) attaches the self to its Divine source, while the last "I shall be" (of understanding) grounds it within creation. The first corresponds to the deepening of consciousness while the last corresponds to the settling of consciousness.

Chapter 3

1. See *Tanya*, end of chapter 3.

2. In Kabbalah, these three are called choice (*bechirah*), desire (*chefetz*), and drive (*ratzon*). The distinct manifestations of the three levels of conscious will clearly point to a division based on the hierarchy of the *sefirot*: the faith-based power of choice corresponds to the cognitive *sefirot* (crown, wisdom and understanding); the pleasure-based longing of desire corresponds to the *sefirot* of the emotive realm (loving-kindness, might and beauty); and the raw force of drive corresponds to the *sefirot* of the instinctive realm (victory, thanksgiving, foundation and kingdom).

As stated, all three levels of conscious choice are manifestations of super-conscious will, as present in each one of the three heads of the super-conscious crown. Choice is clearly the most essential expression of our free will. This is reflected by the fact that throughout the Bible the Hebrew verb *livchor*, "to choose" is rendered in Aramaic as *itre'i*, from the Aramaic for "will." See *Or Torah*, *Shmot*, p. 2792.

3. See "Choice and Intellect" (p. 145).

4. The first appearance of a word in the Bible sets the scene for all of its subsequent appearances. The word desire appears for the first time in Genesis 34:19. There it describes the passionate desire of Shechem, the son of Chamor (the ruler of the city Shechem) for Dinah, the daughter of Jacob. Even though it appears there in a negative context, we nonetheless learn from it that desire is indeed the deepest expression of love, in the sense of emotional longing for some form of gratification, whether positive or negative, achievable only through external experience.

5. See "Will-power" (p. 147).

6. Ascribing the source of all three manifestations of free will—choice, desire and drive—to the super-conscious crown prompts us to search for an illustration of the matrix of free will therein. In fact, by taking the roots of the original Hebrew words for these three manifestations, choice (בחר), desire (חפץ), and drive (רצה) and assembling them one on top of the other as they would be conceptually ordered within the super-conscious, we can find a meditatively inspiring depiction of the matrix of free will within the crown:

faith/choice	ר	ח	ב
pleasure/desire	צ	פ	ח
will/drive	ה	צ	ר

One can see that the three roots read the same whether read horizontally or vertically.

7. Desire implies a somewhat greater degree of autonomy, insofar as it derives from the essentially self-sufficient realm of pleasure. But, only choice can be realized from a truly autonomous position of selfhood, as the wholly transcendent sphere of faith inspires it. Hence choice affirms, from a distance, the innate identification between self and outer reality, while leaving the forces of desire and drive to provide the necessary ballast for transforming that abstract identification into a felt imperative.

8. Psalms 119:30.

9. *Hilchot Yesodei Hatorah* 2:10.

10. Rabbi Shneur Zalman of Liadi in the *Tanya* (chapter 2), describing the nature of the soul's attachment to its Divine source, states that "the soul of every Israelite is derived from the Almighty's thought and wisdom." Elsewhere, in *Likutei Torah* (*Ha'azinu* 78a; *Shir Hashirim* 44d) he further explains that the verse from Isaiah (55:8), "for My thoughts are not your thoughts, nor are My paths your paths," implies that incompatible thought

processes are the result of incompatible paths of life. The simple conclusion is that one has to commit oneself to "walk in the paths of God"—to emulate His attributes—if one hopes to understand His "thoughts" and wisdom. On a deeper level, the verse suggests that one who follows the "path of faith," which is the path chosen by God, can hope to access His "thought."

11. This is reflected in the verse "for God is a God of *de'ot*" (II Samuel 2:3). The word *de'ot* is the plural form of *da'at*—knowledge, or consciousness. The verse thus alludes to the unification within God's own "knowledge" of both higher and lower consciousness.

12. There are truths that are grounded in subjective faith, such as those we refer to as axiomatic, and truths that are grounded in reason. While the latter are those generally associated with the word truth (*emet*), the former are alluded to by its grammatical root that is also the root of faith (*emunah*).

The faith underlying truth can be thought of as feminine truth, while truth-proper denotes the masculine aspect of truth. This is reflected in the Kabbalistic assertion (see *Zohar* III:198b) that, "He [God's "masculine" aspect] is truth, and She [His "feminine" aspect] is faith" (*ihu emet ve'ihi emunah*).

13. Deuteronomy 7:6; see also Ibid. 14:2. In the Bible, the only other instances of Divine super-rational choice of particular souls are His choice of Aaron and the priestly class (Ibid. 18:5; 21:5), the Levites (I Chronicles 15:2), and King David and his descendants (II Samuel 6:21)—all key elements in the fulfillment of the covenant initiated at Mt. Sinai. See "God's Essential Choices" (p. 149).

14. In the same way, we find that God's "choice" of the Nation of Israel was questioned on the basis of their external similarity to other nations: "these are idol worshippers and these are idol worshippers" (*Vayikra Rabbah* 21:4). Given this "external

resemblance" of the Jew to the non-Jew, only Divine choice could indeed differentiate and decide between seemingly similar realities. By analogy, we may say that it was the super-rational power of faith that God had in the Jewish people (regardless of appearances) that provided the justification for His choice.

[In passing, we should clarify that according to Kabbalah and Chassidut, the inner essence of the Jew does not need to be chosen by God, for it is a part of Him. This idea is expressed in *Tanya* (chapter 49) where the liturgical phrase, "and You chose us over every other people and tongue," is explained as referring to God's choice of Israel's *material* body, which resembles in its materiality the bodies of the nations of the world.]

15. See "The Linguistic Root of Choice" (p. 152).

16. Deuteronomy 30:19 and also Ibid. 30:15.

17. This is evident from the use of the word *haba* (literally, "coming") in describing this eternal realm—a word that can simultaneously mean "came," "comes," and "will come."

The expression World-to-Come also appears in reference to the perfected state of creation subsequent to the resurrection of the dead. This is the World-to-Come that the Talmud in *Sanhedrin* (chapter 11) discusses in regard to who will or will not share in its perfection. This is the same historical age occasionally referred to as the Future-to-Come (*La'atid Lavo*). When it arrives, the supra-temporal World-to-Come to which we refer in our text (the disembodied "realm of soul") will be incorporated into the material realm, a truly miraculous state reflecting God's Infinite Light more clearly than it appears even in the eternal, supra-temporal World-to-Come.

18. Hence it is the realm that is accessed when one does complete repentance (*teshuvah*, literally, "return to God"), a process that the sages teach us has the power to transform past iniquities into present and future merits.

Both repentance and the World-to-Come are identified in Kabbalah with the *sefirah* of understanding immediately preceding the *sefirah* of knowledge. (Our world, on the other hand, is associated with the seven *sefirot* that follow knowledge.) Without the power of choice associated with knowledge, one could not access the World-to-Come of understanding. At the same time, it is the attachment to understanding that allows knowledge to exercise transcendent choice.

19. According to Kabbalah, the two super-conscious powers of faith and pleasure combine to make up the supreme *partzuf* of the crown, *atik yomin*. The first three *sefirot* of this *partzuf* reside in faith, while its seven lower *sefirot* reside in pleasure.

20. See the introduction to *Muda'oot Tivit*.

21. Indeed, the root ברר is found in the Bible to denote the act of choosing (see Ecclesiastes 3:18 and elsewhere). In rabbinic sources, this meaning is even more pronounced, as in the concept of selection (*borer*), related to the laws of Shabbat. Later yet, the word *brerah* became synonymous with choice in the sense of an option.

22. See "Knowledge and Understanding" (p. 153).

23. Psalms 40:6.

24. These two "sensors" are referred to in Kabbalah as the *chasadim* ("forces of loving-kindness") and the *gevurot* ("forces of strength or might") of consciousness. The *chasadim* correspond to the five *sefirot* (within knowledge) that tend to affirm lower reality, while the *gevurot* correspond to the five *sefirot* (within knowledge) that tend to negate lower reality.

In *Sefer Yetzirah*, these two constellations within consciousness are also referred to as "the depth of goodness" (*omek tov*)—corresponding to the *chasadim*—and "the depth of evil" (*omek ra*)—corresponding to the *gevurot*. Together with "space" (*olam*) and "time" (*shanah*), they chart a third phase of reality called "soul" (*nefesh*) that expresses itself through the mediation of values. Between them, these three phases include five dimensions (3 for space, 1 for time and 1 for soul) corresponding to the *heh* (= 5) added to the name of the traditional author of *Sefer Yetzirah*— Abraham. The 10 *sefirot* are then the extremities of these 5 dimensions of reality.

25. The term direct light is employed in Kabbalah to describe the descending vector of light (associated with the forces of loving-kindness), which draws Divine goodness into creation, thus affirming it as a positive reality. The reflected light describes the ascending vector of light associated with the forces of strength, which seek to raise creation back to its Divine source by disaffirming its negative elements. See also "Clarification and Selection" (p. 155).

26. See also "Clarification and Selection" (p. 155).

27. In fact, the process continues even in the afterlife, where it is said that souls ascend through the infinite levels of the heavenly Eden.

28. Genesis 2:9.

29. See also "Naivite vs Natural Consciousness" (p. 157).

30. Genesis 2:15.

31. Ibid. 2:17.

32. Although God formulated His directive as a command to refrain from eating from the Tree of Knowledge, His desire that Adam and Eve partake of the Tree of Life is implicit in the words preceding that directive (Genesis 2:16-17): "From all the trees of the garden [including the Tree of Life] you shall surely eat, but you shall not eat from the Tree of Knowledge of Good and Evil...." (See also the commentary of *Ibn-Ezra* on this verse.)

33. *Mei Hashiloach.*

34. Genesis 2:17.

35. Assimilating the knowledge of good and evil allowed Adam and Eve to experience their choices and actions as the results of their own subjective frame of reference. Unlike the transcendentally-inspired choice identified with the Tree of Life, the clarifications of physical reality associated with the Tree of Knowledge arise from the known quantities of conscious experience. Through human consciousness, countless relationships between the diverse elements of creation are inferred and articulated; each one hinging on the subset of reality that presents itself at the moment. This relativity is what makes consciousness nothing more than the field upon which the ongoing process of value-clarification occurs.

36. Rashi to Deuteronomy 30:15.

37. Genesis 2:9. See also the commentary of Nachmanides on this verse, which sees this as the implicit teaching of Onkelos' Aramaic rendition of the verse.

38. Genesis 3:2-3.

39. The numerical value of the word for life (חַיִּים) is 68, which equals 4 times the value of good (טוֹב), 17; in other words, the average value of each of the four letters of life (חַיִּים) is good (טוֹב).

Similarly, the numerical value of the Hebrew phrase for "the Tree of Knowledge of Good and Evil" (עֵץ הַדַּעַת טוֹב וָרָע), 932 is 4 times the value of the phrase for the Tree of Life (עֵץ הַחַיִּים), 233. As the original Hebrew of the Tree of Knowledge of Good and Evil is comprised of 4 words, the average value of each word is the value of the Tree of Life. Hence, we see how these two existential symbols are intertwined numerically.

Faith (אֱמוּנָה) is the ultimate super-conscious root of both of these modes. Its numerical value, 102, equals 6 times good (טוֹב), 17 (thereby embracing all six of its permutations), or 1½ times life

(חַיִּים). One and a half in Kabbalah (the whole and the half), alludes to secret of the union of male and female.

40. *Zohar* I:35b, and elsewhere.

41. The prayer for dew (*tefilat tal*) and prayer for rain (*tefilat geshem*) recited on the seventh day of Passover and *Shemini Atzeret* (the eighth day of *Sukot*), respectively.

42. The firm decision, which results from the product of one's choice being subjected to clarification, is referred to in our model as decision, and is associated with the *sefirah* of foundation, the last of the six forces of clarification. The word *hachlatah*, "decision," is as we will see, based on the same root as the word *muchlat* ("absolute")—thereby alluding to the absolutist character restored to one's choices once the process of clarification has been allowed to run its course.

Chapter 4

1. See also "Knowledge and the Chambers of the Heart" (p. 159).

2. Following the saying of our sages (*Avot* 4:1): "Who is *strong*? He who can *restrain* his inclinations."

3. "Behaviorist" here is used interchangeably with "instinctual."

4. These powers are called in Kabbalah benevolence (*chesed*), judgment (*din*) and mercy (*rachamim*), as explained above.

5. The forces of judgment support this objective as well, insofar as they guarantee that the life-force we wish to invest in the

world is properly directed, and not squandered or usurped by another for unwarranted purposes. Moreover, the repudiation associated with judgment often serves to prepare the negated part of reality to be re-embraced by the soul—though this effect usually remains unseen.

6. The best example of this is found in Abraham's instructions to his servant Eliezer to choose a wife for his son Isaac from among his kin. Eliezer is told that, rather than make any concessions or compromises with regard to the condition that the chosen woman be from Abraham's kin, he should see himself as relieved of his mission (See Genesis 24).

7. The appropriate paradigm for illustrating how the decision-making capacity of consciousness operates when guided chiefly by the mind is that of the judiciary process. It is nevertheless important to note that even in the objective assessment of reality that accompanies legal decisions, one is obligated to seek an affirmative justification (*hatzdakah*) of the defendant, as intimated in the Torah's commandment (Leviticus 19:15): "Judge your friend with justice [*tzedek*]"—interpreted as meaning that one should always judge his fellow man positively (see *Avot* 1:6). Indeed, the assumption underlying all cognitive assessments of creation is that of essential worthiness. This is the baseline from which one proceeds to judge the specifics of any situation.

This affirmative bias that is built into the "scales of justice" is a manifestation of the association between judgment (*din*) and mercy (*rachamim*), which, as we have indicated, lies along the central axis of the sefirotic tree but nevertheless seeks to promote the force of benevolence (*chesed*) on the right.

8. In the *Zohar* (III:224a), the conscious control of emotion by intellect is referred to as "the brain ruling the heart." The more sublime interaction to which we now refer is expressed in Chassidut as "the heart's interior ruling the brain."

9. That is why, when the *sefirot* are situated in context of the human body, knowledge is usually identified with the neck region: in the interior, from the brain stem to the spinal cord; on the exterior, along the extent of the neck. As such, it is situated at the crossroads between the mind (head) and the emotive center (the torso, seat of the heart).

10. 2:6 and 8:3.

11. *Sotah* 47a and *Sanhedrin* 107b.

These two forces of rejection and invitation correspond to objectivity (*nekiyut hada'at*) and affinity (*kiruv hada'at*). The source of rejection and invitation in Kabbalistic terms are the five *chassadim* (the plural form of loving-kindness, leaning to the right) and the five *gevurot* (the plural form of strength, leaning to the left) that make up the *sefirah* of knowledge. Though from the idiom it would seem that rejection/objectivity (the five *gevurot*) expresses itself before invitation/affinity (the five *chassadim*), it is clear that in relation to our thought or intent it is the five *chassadim*, the desire to draw near, that motivate the process. Whereas, when it comes to action, our left-leaning powers of objectivity precede the right-leaning powers of affinity.

In Kabbalah, the balance of right and left is the most essential indication of rectification. It is rectified consciousness, *da'at*, that at once "knows" the secret of balance and produces the state of balance in the soul.

While the five *chassadim* arouse mercy on the other, the *gevurot* break the external shell around the other that hides its Divine content. In the Book of Judges (8:16) we find the verb "to know" (*vayoda*) in the sense of "to break." See *Or Torah Shemot*, pages 1105-6.

12. Appraisal is indeed strongly related to judgment, which is usually identified with the *sefirah* of strength, also called judgment (*din*). Nonetheless, in Kabbalah we learn that the inner essence of

beauty, the *sefirah* associated with appraisal, is itself judgment (*mishpat*)—not judgment as a quality, but rather judgment in the sense of the judicial process.

This can be explained by noting that the cornerstone of the Jewish judicial process is compassion (*rachamim*), the inner force of beauty. Our sages identified the reason for the destruction of Jerusalem with the lack of compassion in the judicial process (*Baba Metzia* 30b). And, in the introduction to the *Tikunei Zohar* (*Patach Eliyahu*) we find the identity: "judgment—[is] compassion."

13. This predisposition reflects the fact that beauty, though positioned beneath knowledge along the central axis of the *sefirot* leans to the right side of loving-kindness. For this reason, the *sefirah* of beauty is also identified with the quality of compassion that expresses itself in the tendency of appraisal to "judge positively."

One can recognize these various forces in the Halachic laws that pertain to jurisprudence. Judges are required to first receive the litigants and establish a dialogue with them based on a proper affective balance of affinity and objectivity. So as not to intimidate or inhibit either party, the judges must take care to respond to each of the litigants with equal empathy. Only in the subsequent stage of deliberation, identifiable as appraisal, do the categories of legal principle assert themselves (reflecting the ability of the *sefirah* of beauty to invoke the theoretical conclusions of prior knowledge). This, of course, does not mean that legal knowledge is unimportant to the hearing; it simply suggests that such knowledge should not compromise the essential relationship that must form between a judge and his litigants if the full scope of their positions is to be grasped. See *Shulchan Aruch, Choshen Mishpat* 17:1 and 5:10.

14. The inner quality of victory is confidence (*bitachon*), the trait one needs in order to emerge victorious when battling for change. In Hebrew, the word for "victory" (*netzach*) also means "eternity."

Conceptually, eternity seems to negate the notion of change so crucial to process. It would therefore appear to contradict the essence of the *sefirah* of victory—the confident promotion of change, as described above. To resolve this apparent contradiction we need to emphasize that the transformations sought by victory are actually stages in an infinite spiritual ascent that reflects the striving of the soul toward "the Eternity of Israel" (*Netzach Yisrael*), as God Himself is called in I Samuel 15:29. Thus, though there is a "process" of sorts involved, every step of the way is informed by the transcendent unchanging character of the Eternity of Israel, which is its goal.

15. The relationship between thanksgiving and its corollary state of surrender can be described in two ways: 1) as a referant for Divine majesty or splendor, thanksgiving refers to the aura one draws down upon oneself when in a state of higher surrender; 2) etymologically, thanksgiving serves as the root of the Hebrew word for "acknowledgment" (*hodayah*), thus also alluding to the role of self-resignation in allowing one to acknowledge God's infinite greatness.

16. Unlike the force of intuition that we earlier identified with the *sefirah* of wisdom, the intuitive powers of victory and thanksgiving express themselves in emotive rather than cognitive fashion. The Kabbalistic use of the Midrashic metaphor "counseling kidneys" (*klayot yo'atzot*) to describe these two forces suggests a parallel with the popular notion of "gut feeling."

17. The inner quality associated with thanksgiving is sincerity (*temimut*), an integral aspect of all commitment, and a property exalted in the Torah for its ability to render one immune to the irrelevant thoughts that tend to distract from a desired goal. The difficulty in expressing one's innate sincerity, due to the unrelenting pretensions of human character, is conveyed by the verse: "God has made men straight, yet they seek out countless contrivances" (Ecclesiastes 7:29).

The initial letters of the three words, "seek out countless contrivances" (בִּקְשׁוּ חִשְּׁבֹנוֹת רַבִּים) spell the word (בחר), which is the infinitive form of the verb "to choose." The final letters of this phrase permute to spell death (מָוֶת). God places before us the two opposites of life and death and tells us to choose life (Deuteronomy 30:19). To walk straight with sincerity (*temimut*) as God made us, is choosing life, whereas to seek out countless contrivances, to walk crooked, is to choose the opposite.

One very fine example of sincerity is that of Nachshon, the prince of the tribe of Judah (יְהוּדָה), whose very name comes from the same root as "thanksgiving" (הוֹד). Nachshon was the first to venture into the Red Sea before it parted. It is said that his determination to proceed into the waters came from a vision of Mt. Sinai and the receiving of the Torah that Moses had implanted in his consciousness. At an inner level, this vision is shared by every Jew and imparts the same sense of determination and readiness to act.

18. This tendency reflects victory's position directly beneath the affirmative emotive *sefirah* of loving-kindness along the right axis of the *sefirot*, as well as its following the *sefirah* of beauty that also relatively leans toward the right and hence encourages affirmation.

19. The Hebrew word *hachra'ah* that we translated as "resolve" also appears in rabbinic sources (*Baba Batra* 88b) in another sense directly related to our discussion. With regard to the use of weights and measures, in those places that it is customary to do so: "…One is obligated to *weigh down* [the scale holding the measure] an additional fist-breadth." The practice of "weighing down" or *hachra'ah* is clearly to the advantage of the buyer and serves as a particularly astute metaphor for the power of victory to "tip the scales" following the stage of appraisal (*shikul hada'at*, which can also be translated as the "weighing of consciousness") in favor of affirming the outer attachments acquired by experience.

The practice of "weighing down" also pertains to the Kabbalistic description of the two *sefirot* of victory and thanksgiving as the two bowls of a scale. Victory is pictured as the winner—the heavier bowl that descends, while thanksgiving (which can also be translated as "acknowledgment") is pictured as the loser or conceder—the lighter bowl that ascends (*Introduction to Tikunei Zohar, Patach Eliahu*).

20. The dynamic of concurrence is evident as well in the requirement that a court must render a legal decision unanimously, even though that decision may only be the result of a majority opinion (see *Shulchan Aruch, Choshen Mishpat* 19:1-2).

21. These are represented by the *sefirot* of wisdom through thanksgiving.

22. The Ba'al Shem Tov (see *Keter Shem Tov* 16) would refer to foundation as the "aroused [literally, 'living'] organ" (*evar chai*) of the soul, borrowing a term that is generally applied to its anatomical counterpart in order to express the vitality associated with one's creative impulses.

23. Foundation is aligned beneath the crown, knowledge and beauty, along the central axis of the sefirotic tree. The central axis (descending from crown to kingdom) can be understood as an evolutionary continuum of the integrative faculties of the soul. Knowledge and foundation then correspond to the origin and end-point of the affective realm, whose "body" is centrally represented by beauty.

24. "Random circumstance" (*mikreh*) is associated with the "spilling" or wasting of the vital seed of life (as in the idiom *mikreh laylah*; Deuteronomy 23:11). It is also referred to as "blemishing the covenant" (*pegam habrit*).

It follows therefore that indecisiveness reflects a personality whose covenant (associated with the *sefirah* of foundation) is blemished. Such a person's rectification (*tikun pegam habrit*) is to learn—generally by means of the inspiration given to him by a Torah sage to whom he is devoted—to act generously toward others with inwardly aroused decisiveness. Every soul has the ability to be decisive. Indecisiveness is the result of one's innermost spiritual potency having receded and disappeared into the depths of unconsciousness. Rectifying the blemish of the covenant (*tikun pgam habrit*) is akin to "calling" one's essential potency to reappear (see the Rebbe Rashab's collection of talks *Torat Shalom*, p. 172-3).

25. See also "If I Am Not For Myself…" (p. 161).

26. *Otzar Hapitgamim.*

27. Psalms 113:9.

28. The relationship between one's final decision and its verbal expression is depicted by the metaphor of "a seal within a seal," usually employed in Kabbalah to describe the attachment of foundation to kingdom (see *Avodah Zara* 29b; *Pri Etz Chayim, Sha'ar Halulav*, chapter 4; *Kehilat Yaakov*, s.v.). The inner seal is that of foundation—the private decision that one makes—while the outer seal is the words one uses to express that decision to the other.

29. Based on the verse "For the word of a king is authority" (Ecclesiastes 8:4); "king" here alludes to the *sefirah* of kingdom.

30. The identification of speech as a central element of our identity as human beings and as a symbol of our kingdom or dominion in the world is made explicit in the Onkelos Aramaic translation of the verse "and man became a living soul," (Genesis 2:7) which it renders as: "and the soul in man became an uttering spirit."

31. Psalms 19:3. The root of the word for expression (יְחַוֶּה) in this verse is חוה which spells Eve in Hebrew. This root appears only five more times in the Bible, all of them in the Book of Job. The numerical value of Job (אִיּוֹב) is equal to that of Eve (חַוָּה), 19

(note that the phrase cited above from Psalms is from chapter 19). In all but one of these appearances, the word is contextually linked with the grammatical root of the Hebrew word for knowledge (*da'at*).

32. Rashi explicitly states that "expression" (*yechaveh*) means "to verbally relate."

33. Genesis 3:20. Insofar as kingdom is normally identified as a feminine force, the association of expression with Eve, the first woman, is pertinent to its association with the concept of verbal expressiveness. The inherent connection between the two associations is evident from the statement of the sages that "ten measures of speech descended upon the world, of which woman took nine" (*Kidushin* 49b).

34. See endnote 22 above. Because of the vitality of the procreative seed it is referred to as living seed (*zera chai*). From this vitality comes the phrase "a living and lasting seed" (*za'ra chaya ve'kayama*; from Shabbat Day liturgy). In both cases it is implied that for creative expression to be complete and lasting, there must be vitality at the level of foundation in the decision process.

35. Genesis 4:1.

36. It is fitting to note here, as well, that the dynamic interplay between silence and speech represents, according to the Ba'al Shem Tov, the Kabbalistic energy of the electrum (*chashmal*) referred to in Ezekiel's vision of the heavenly chariot (Ezekiel 1:4, 27). Compounding the syllables *chash*, meaning "silence," and *mal*, meaning "speech", produces the word *chashmal*. Together these two qualities comprise the dialectic that serves as the basis of all Divine service.

37. There are various guidelines for resolving differences of Halachic opinion between the sages of the *Mishnah*, based on the description of their teachings (see *Gittin* 67a). One of these is that the opinion of Rabbi Yossi (ben Chalafta) is always accepted

because, in the idiom of the Talmud, "he justifies/rationalizes his ruling" (*nimuko imo*; ibid. and *Eiruvin* 51a). According to our analysis this is an example of how vitality promotes a decision that can be lucidly explained and justified. Vitality, as mentioned above, depends on the rectification of foundation, associated with the procreative organ. Regarding his rectification in this respect, Rabbi Yossi is related to have said that his whole life he never looked at his procreative organ (*Shabbat* 118b).

Chapter 5

1. Genesis 4:1. An additional allusion is found in the verse: "Without knowledge the soul is not good" (Proverbs 19:2). One may liken the meaning of the words "not good" in this verse to the same words in the verse: "It is not good for man to be alone, I will make for him a helpmate to complement him" (Genesis 2:18). Thus, it is the absence of knowledge/consciousness, as implied by the verse in Proverbs that is responsible for the "not good" state of being alone.

2. See "Knowledge and Possession" (p. 162).

3. The affinity between possession and the idea of enclothement is further reinforced by the similarity of the Hebrew words for "possession" (*kinyan*), and "nest" (*ken*), and "garment" or "rectification" (*tikun*); both *ken* and *tikun* allude to the restorative effect of enclothing oneself in a protective element. All three ideas are alluded to in the verse: "Is He not your Father Who has possessed you?" (Deuteronomy 32:6). Rashi, in his commentary on this verse, combines all three meanings: "'Who

has possessed you,' Who has nested you in rocks and on strong land, Who has bedecked you in all manner of refinement."

4. The above verse from Genesis may now be interpreted thus: "And Adam knew [i.e., enclothed himself—body, mind, and soul—within] Eve his wife. And she conceived [i.e., absorbed his essence] and bore Cain. And she said: I have possessed [i.e., enclothed myself within] a man [her son] with the help, and in the presence, of God."

5. *Tanya*, Chapter 3.

6. Antithetical to the experience of recognition (*hakarah*) is the linguistically related state of alienation (*nikur*). Both are derived from the same root, נקר, which implies a weak identification between one's inner self and the outer milieu.

7. Genesis 2:18-20.

8. Ibid. 2:23. This verse possesses some remarkable numerical allusions to the subject at hand. In the Hebrew original it has 15 words and 57 letters. The Hebrew word for choice (בְּחִירָה) equals 225, or 15^2 and the Hebrew word for decision (הַחְלָטָה) equals 57. The numerical signature of the verse (calculated by multiplying the number of words by the number of letters, 15 times 57) is 855, which is equivalent to Adam (אָדָם), 45, multiplied by 19, the numerical value of Eve (חַוָה).

9. Rashi (citing *Yevamot* 63a) explains that "at last" means that man cohabited with every animal but was not satisfied until he cohabited with Eve. Applying a deeper dimension of understanding to Rashi's explanation, cohabitation here is meant as a metaphor for relations of a mental sort, whereby Adam attempted to unite with and possess other creatures through the apprehension of their true natures.

10. Genesis 3:20.

11. The Hebrew term for proper noun, *shem ha'etzem*, literally means "name of the essence." But interestingly, the word for

essence (*etzem*) also means "bone," alluding to the description of Adam's helpmate as "bone of my bone...."

12. Genesis 3:20.

Chapter 6

1. Pages 16ff.

2. The excessive self-sufficiency associated with the protracted state of singleness may be the result of a maladapted super-conscious identification with the initial gender-duality of Adam at the time of his creation. This identification is alluded to by the fact that the numerical value of the words in Hebrew for bachelor (רַוָּק) and woman (אִשָּׁה) are both equal to 306, whereas the values of the words for bachelorette (רַוָּקָה) and man (אִישׁ) both equal 311.

3. Although one may find these character types in members of either sex, the identification of pleasure and will as the respective male and female principles of super-consciousness seems to suggest that the first syndrome is more typical of men and the latter of women.

4. The word *hamtanah*, which expresses the idea of patient waiting, is cognate to the word *metinut*, denoting moderation. *Metinut* is what endows consciousness with the deliberate patience and attentiveness that is so crucial to the proper apprehension of an other's true nature.

The Ba'al Shem Tov described rectified consciousness as possessing the quality of agility-tempered-by-moderation (*zerizut bemetinut*)—an idiom that beautifully expresses the kind of consciousness that, while excitable, remains modulated, and, while energized, is free of compulsion. The agility or zeal (*zerizut*) of consciousness has its source in the impetuous will of super-consciousness—will, or *ratzon* in Hebrew, being cognate to run, or *ratz*. The moderation (*metinut*) of consciousness stems from the steadfast faith (*emunah*) of super-consciousness, their two-letter sub-root, מן, being the same.

5. Job 36:2.

6. The Hebrew root of expression, חוה, which often appears in conjunction with knowledge, is also the root of the word *achaveka* in the above verse, which means "I will show you." Hence, both of knowledge's extremities—its crown and its kingdom—are intimated in the verse from *Job*.

This root appears six times in the Bible, five of which explicitly link it with knowledge (Psalms 19:3; Job 32:6, 10, and 17; Ibid 36:2). The four references from the Book of Job are all associated with the figure of Elihu, Job's compassionate ally, who patiently endures the empty moralizing of Job's other comrades before communicating his own supportive perspective regarding Job's suffering.

7. Genesis 2:21.

8. The three letter root of "deep sleep," (רדם), shares the same two-letter root (דָם) with both Adam (אָדָם) and silence (דְמָמָה).

9. Adam is also related to the *sefirah* of crown, mathematically. The letters of Adam (אדם) when spelled out (אלף דלת מם) equal 625, which is also the value of "the crown" (הַכֶּתֶר) or 5^4; this alludes to the crown's correspondence with the 5th, and highest level of the soul known as the singular one (*yechidah*).

10. Genesis 1:26-28.

11. *Ketubot* 8a.

12. Genesis 5:1.

13. Ibid. 2:21-25.

14. For more on this *split* or *separation* see "The Primordial Origins of the Masculine and Feminine" (p. 164).

15. The ideal state of the shared identity of pleasure and will is one of good will, the consummate state of will involved in finding one's true soulmate and alluded to in the verse: "He who has found a woman has found good, and he will elicit the [good] will of God" (Proverbs 14:22).

16. Faith, the highest starta of super-consciousness, promotes a reciprocal reflection between the apparently antithetical male and female super-conscious forces. This idea is alluded to in a Midrash cited by Rashi in his commentary to Exodus 38:8. The Midrash describes the strategy employed by the righteous women of Israel, during the slavery in Egypt, to entice their weary husbands into marital relations. The woman would gaze with her husband into a mirror and then proclaim how much more beautiful she was than he. The contemplation of their joint reflection would, according to the Midrash, arouse the desire of the husband to have relations with his wife.

The bondage of Egypt appears in Kabbalah as a metaphor for the state of the crown in the communal soul of Israel preceding the birth of knowledge at Sinai. The righteous women represent the faith-inspired capacity of female-will to promote the birth of knowledge by enticing male-pleasure with the beauty born of their shared reflection. The sages teach us that it was "in merit of the righteous women," as well as "in merit of faith," that the Jews were delivered from Egypt, thereby alluding to the relationship between the female force of will and the supreme power of faith.

17. Genesis 2:25.

18. A "soulmate" can now be understood as being more than just a kindred spirit, but rather as someone who actually shares one's soul-essence. See "A Whole and a Half" (p. 167).

19. The great exponent of *Chabad* Chassidut, Rabbi Isaac of Homil, views deep sleep (*tardemah*) as the source of those dreams that are capable of being realized.

In Kabbalah, such dreams are attributed to Primordial Man (*Adam Kadmon*), the (human form) prototype of God's primordial design for creation. (As noted above in endnote 9, the two-letter sub-root of *tardemah,* דם, is the same as that of *Adam.*) All the worlds willed into being by the Creator existed first as "dreams" of Primordial Man. In mortal man, the power of "deep sleep" expresses itself through the ability to "translate" (*targum*) one's inner vision into conscious experience. The two words, deep sleep (תַּרְדֵּמָה) and translation (תַּרְגּוּם) possess the same numerical value, 649.

20. Song of Songs 4:9-10, 4:12, 5:1-2. In the first four of these references, the full idiom is "my sister bride" (*achoti kallah*). In the last reference, "my sister" (*achoti*) appears as the first in a string of endearments that reflect various dimensions of the love relationship: "my sister, my companion, my dove, my perfect one." In addition, "sister" (*achot*) appears twice toward the end of the book: "we have a young sister ... what shall we do for our sister..."(Ibid. 8:8). According to the *Targum*, this verse is spoken by the angels in reference to the "bride" of the love song, Israel.

21. Song of Songs 8:1. See also "Fraternity and Marriage" (p. 168).

22. This difference can be compared to that which exists between the two categories of commandments, those referred to as frequent (*tadir*) and those termed more sanctified (*mekudash*). Just as a "frequent commandment" takes precedence over one that is "more sanctified," so does the constancy of fraternity present an advantage over the sanctity of love. The word *kodesh*, "sanctity," is seen by the sages to be short for *yekud esh*, or "set on fire." Similarly, it is love's flame-like nature that renders it prone to

fluctuation (as reflected in the suspension of its physical expression during periods of ritual impurity).

23. See also "Eternal Fraternity" (p. 170).

24. Genesis 2:25. See "Fraternity and Unity" (p. 172).

25. The letters אח also form the primal root of "splicing" or "fusing" (*ichui*), alluding to the fusion of male and female within the original body of Adam. The power to restore fusion is associated with the (name of the) prophet Achiyah. Though Achiyah was the prophet who forecasted the schism between the kingdoms of Judah and Israel by rending King Jeraboam's cloak into twelve pieces (see I Kings 11:29), giving ten pieces to Jeraboam and the remainder to the House of David, he is also expected to herald the restoration of a single Jewish commonwealth with the coming of the Messiah. In so doing, Achiyah, whose name derives from the word for fusion (*ichui*), will stitch together the remnants of Israel into a "cloak of many colors," thus restoring the fraternity between Joseph and his brothers.

26. See "Fraternity and Love" (p. 173).

27. The verb *dom* appears in various forms throughout the Bible, often alluding to a state of arrest or paralysis, as in the verse (Joshua 10:12): "Sun in *Givon*, stand still [*dom*]." Perhaps this is the reason that the color red (*adom*), also derived from the two-letter sub-root דם, is commonly used for stop signals.

Dom is also used to describe Aaron's silence upon witnessing the death of his two sons, Nadav and Avihu, at the hand of the Almighty: "And Aaron was silent [*va'yidom Aharon*]" (Leviticus 10:3).

Just as the silence of the mourner (who is referred to as "one without a mouth") has the power to transform travail (צָרָה) into light (צֹהַר) so too can one discover consciousness through the silence of super-consciousness.

28. Psalms 62:1. Later, in Psalms 62:6, this pronouncement virtually repeats itself: "For God alone, my soul waits in silence; for from Him comes my hope." Whereas the first verse reflects the perspective of pleasure, whose obsession with super-conscious experience requires an extreme force of "salvation" to impel it into consciousness, the second verse reflects the perspective of will that needs only hope in order to pursue its native inclination to enter consciousness.

29. Genesis 1:26.

30. The word for "shadow" (*tzel*), is indeed the two letter root of the word for "image" (*tzelem*)—the image of God in which man was created.

In Psalms (121:5) we find that "God is your shadow." Just as we are God's shadow within the created realm, so God appears to us as our shadow, to protect and save us (the root "to save" [*n-tz-l*], derives from the same two letter root as "shadow"). "God is our shadow" also in the sense that He relates to us just as we relate to our fellow man.

31. The emulation of God is mandated by the commandment: "You shall walk in His ways" (Deuteronomy 28:9). This commandment, referred to as the obligation "to be like [*lehidamot*, from the same root as that of *kidmuteinu*, 'similar to our likeness'] Him [the Creator]"—is expounded by the sages as implying that "just as He is merciful so be you merciful, just as He is forgiving... so be you."

The idea of emulating the Almighty was corrupted by the Babylonian King Nebuchadnezzar, who proclaimed: "I will ascend above the heights of cloud; I will become like [*adameh*] the Supreme One" (Isaiah 14:14). In Chassidic writings, however, the phrase "I will become like the Supreme One" appears in its reconstructed sense as the positive desire to emulate God.

32. See "Image and Likeness" (p. 175).

33. This is the implicit meaning of the rabbinic statement found in the Midrash: "There is no woman more fitting than she who does the will of her husband" (*Tanchuma,* 9). The words "does the will" (*osah retzon*) can be understood as "fashions the will," thereby alluding to her role as that of cultivating her husband's super-conscious will.

34. This idea is a creative interpretation of the Divine judgment directed at Eve: "And to your husband shall be your passion; and he shall rule (*yimshol*) over you" (Genesis 3:16). The words "and he shall rule over you" may be interpreted as "he will formulate his *parables* about you," implying Eve's ability to model, in Adam's mind, the abstract essence of his own being.

In the Book of Proverbs, the woman is frequently employed as an allegorical symbol (see Proverbs 1:20-33 et. al.) of either good or evil in life. The writings of the Prophets are also replete with references to the people of Israel as the beloved, though often estranged, "wife" of the Almighty.

35. Psalms 104:2.

36. The Midrash refers to God's Infinite Light as "His Name": "Prior to the world being created, there was only God and His Name" (*Pirkei D'Rabbi Eliezer* chapter 3). The word for "His Name" (שְׁמוֹ) in Hebrew is numerically equivalent to the word for will (רָצוֹן), 346, reinforcing the correspondence between the transcendent light that gave birth to creation and the super-conscious force that produces consciousness.

37. Genesis 3:21.

38. *Midrash Bereishit Rabbah* 20:12.

39. The ratio of the numerical values of light (אוֹר), 207, to skin (עוֹר), 276, is three to four. In Kabbalah, three represents the third created realm, the world of formation, of which it is said, "He forms light" (Morning service liturgy). Likewise, four represents the fourth, lowest created realm, the world of action,

the world of shells (קְלִיפוֹת) or "skin" that conceals the light of the Creator.

40. *Tanya, Sha'ar Hayichud Veha'emunah*, chapters 8-9.

41. This is reflected in the verse describing the anticipation of Abraham's servant, Eliezer, upon encountering a potential mate for his master's son, Isaac: "And the man wondered at her, silently waiting to know if God had made his journey successful or not" (Genesis 24:21). The phrase "silently waiting to know" (*macharish lada'at*) alludes to the connection between the silence of super-consciousness and the anticipation of future consciousness.

42. See I Kings 19:12; Psalms 107:29.

Related to the "the sound of subtle silence" (*kol demamah dakah*) is the "the voice of my beloved knocking" (*kol dodi dofek*) found in Song of Songs 5:2. Both idioms possess the identical initials: *k-d-d* (קדד). In the second idiom the intimation of rhythm is pronounced. The "knocking" of the groom on the door of the bride represents God's urging of the soul to awaken from its slumber in super-consciousness so that it might enter the light of consciousness and there sanctify God's Name.

43. See "Silent Speech" (p. 177).

44. See "The Living-Uttering Spirit" (p. 179).

45. Psalms 83:2.

46. *Berachot* 57b. A "beautiful dwelling" and "beautiful furnishings" are also identified here as capable of expanding one's consciousness. The attractiveness of one's home and one's furnishings is ultimately determined by the woman who cares for them. Thus, the "beautiful woman" is the prime facilitator of the expansion of consciousness.

The sum of the numerical values of woman (אִשָּׁה, 306), dwelling (דִּירָה, 219), and furnishings (כֵּלִים, 100) is 625 or 25^2. The initials of these three words *alef* (א), *dalet* (ד) and *kaf* (כ) together equal 25 the square root of 625, which itself is 5^2.

Note also that 625 equals "the crown" (הַכֶּתֶר), which equals *Adam* spelled in full: אלף דלת מם.

The initial letters of woman (א) and dwelling (ד) together with the final letter of "furnishings" (ם) spell Adam (אדם). Thus, the *alef* (א) of Adam corresponds to the *alef* of woman, and as the first letter of a word is its essential, all-inclusive component, we have a further indication that the "beautiful woman" is the prime facilitator of her husband's expansion of consciousness.

47. Genesis 1:28.

48. Isaiah 45:18.

49. *Ta'anit* 26b, 31a; *Yerushalmi Ta'anit* 4:7 (26a-b).

Chapter 7

1. *Ta'anit* (in *Mishnah*) 26b. See also "The Redemptive Power of Love" (p. 181).

2. The *Gemara*'s elaboration of the *Mishnah* (*Ta'anit* 31a) replaces the single entreaty with three separate pleas delivered by sub-groups within the circle.

3. In addition, the *Ein Yaakov* mentions poor and middle-class women together with the unattractive ones as pleading to be chosen "for the sake of heaven."

4. For a discussion of the same account as it appears in the *Yerushalmi Talmud* see "Simple, Double, Triple, and Quadruple Song" (p. 183).

5. See "Virtue, Pleasure, and Profit" (p. 186).

6. Proverbs 31:30.

7. Rashi implies as much in his commentary on the above *Gemara*: "If your children are pedigreed, everyone will leap upon them [for marriage], be they males or females."

8. See chapter 1, endnote 19 and "Virtue, Pleasure, and Profit" (p. 186).

9. The sages portray the Torah firguratively as the "betrothed" of Israel (see *Berachot* 57a on the verse from Deuteronomy 33:4: "'Moses commanded us the Torah, an inheritance of the community of Jacob.' Read not 'inheritance' [*morashah*] but 'betrothed' [*me'urasah*]'").

Thus, the Torah too can be compared to a "betrothed"—to a spiritual guide inspiring his or her soulmate, that is each and every one of us, to service of God in striving to perfect creation, or to rectifiy the world (*tikun olam*), in the idiom of Kabbalah.

10. See pp. 21ff.

11. One of God's motivations (insofar as we can attain a human-centered understanding of them) for creating reality in the first place was His will to act benevolently (*ratzon leheitiv*). See *Shut Chacham Tzvi*, 18; *Shomer Emunim (Hakadmon)*, *Ma'amar Sheni*, chapter 14; *Tanya, Sha'ar Hayichud Ve'ha'emunah* chapter 4. See also *Sod Hashem Liyereiav* chapter 6.

12. Genesis 1:3.

13. *Yevamot* 79a.

14. These three characteristics also appear as the salient traits of our three forefathers: Abraham, Isaac, and Jacob. It is the altruistic spirit—embodied by them and their descendants—which continues to bear testimony to the Divine radiance encompassing creation.

15. In Chassidic discourses it is explained that the term "daughters of Jerusalem" is symbolic of the souls of the nation of Israel.

16. Even according to those who see in the entreaty of the *Mishnah* a composite statement produced by all the classes of maidens later elaborated in the *Gemara*, the single explicit quality referred to in the *Mishnah* remains that of family, reflecting the universal pride taken in the basic lineage of the Jewish soul. Appearing in the context of a *Mishnah*, this intimation reinforces the well-known connection between the words *Mishnah* (מִשְׁנָה) and soul (נְשָׁמָה). Both words are constructed from the identical four letters, a correspondence that is given practical application when *Mishnah* is recited on the annual day of passing (*yahrtzeit*) in order to elevate the soul of the departed.

17. *Etz Chayim, Heichal Alef, Anaf Bet.*

18. Kingdom is the general term used to refer to the Divine emanation whose purpose is to establish a "space" wherein God can exercise sovereignty. When applied to God's Infinite Light (*or ain sof*), kingdom denotes the "area" within God's radiance that He chose as the foundation for His earthly sovereignty. Another term used to refer to this "area" is the higher radiance (*tehiru ila'ah*)—an image that receives poetic expression in Psalms (104:2): "He enwraps Himself in light as if it were a garment" (see *Kedushat Levi* on *Bereishit*).

The process of contraction that takes place in the kingdom of God's Infinite Light comprises three successive contractions, as expounded in the writings of Kabbalah (especially *Emek Hamelech*; see also *Sod Hashem Liyereiav*, chapter 5). Each contraction resulted in a further diminution of God's Infinite Light, until a workable balance was struck between the light's manifestation and its concealment, allowing finite creation. At this point, the creative energy at the core of the God's Infinite Light is referred to as the lower radiance (*tehiru tata'ah*), in contrast to the higher radiance that was manifest before the contraction.

19. In *Sefer Yetzirah* (*Book of Formation*), seven dialectical relationships are associated with the seven lower *sefirot*. The dialectic associated with the *sefirah* of kingdom is grace/ugliness (*chen/ki'ur*). The interplay between these opposing forces is nowhere more evident than in the kingdom of God's Infinite Light. In its pre-contraction state, this kingdom represents the epitome of radiant grace; in its post-contraction state, this same realm becomes corrupted by the ugliness of material reality.

20. Rabbi Yishmael, defending the honor of all Jewish women, asserts the following: "The daughters of Israel are beautiful, but it is poverty that degrades them" (*Nedarim* 66a). Since the Talmud establishes that "there is no poor man, but he who lacks knowledge" (*Nedarim* 41a), Rabbi Yishmael's statement can be taken to infer that it is "poverty" of knowledge (consciousness)—or, unenlightened thinking—that creates an impression of "unsightliness."

21. The contrasting attitudes that we can bring to the encounter with ugliness in the physical world are reflected in the two variant spellings of "unattractive ones," employed by the Babylonian and Jerusalem Talmuds. The Babylonian Talmud spells the Hebrew equivalent with an *ayin* (ע)—כְּעוּרוֹת, however, the Jerusalem Talmud spells the same word with an *alef* (א)—כָּאוּרוֹת.

The Jerusalem Talmud's rare variant suggests an awareness of the "light" (אוֹר) beneath the surface, while the more common spelling found in the Babylonian Talmud, reflects an awareness of only the superficial "skin" (עוֹר) disguising the light within. In Chassidic discourses we find that one who sees only the superficial is likened to a blind person, as the word "ugly" (כָּעוּר) can be read "like a blind person" (כְּעִוֵּר).

22. A process termed in Kabbalah as: "from the thickening of the light the vessels came about" (*me'hitabut ha'orot nithavu ha'kelim*).

23. The suggested association between these two categories, based on their common identification with the profit motive, appears to be supported by their successive appearance in the order of maidens cited by the *Ein Yaakov*, the only source that refers to the wealthy.

24. The particular lineage extolled by the maidens whose families project nobility comes from this common source. The relationship between the communal and individual forms of lineage can be viewed as synonymous with the relationship between God's Infinite Light and the single ray of light. Kabbalah identifies the origin of the ray in the *sefirah* of beauty of the Infinite Light. The *sefirah* of beauty is associated with the attribute of compassion (*rachamim*) embodied by Jacob, the last of our three ancestral forefathers. Jacob begot twelve sons, from whom arose the tribes of Israel, thereby securing his status as the ultimate ancestral source of Jewish lineage.

25. *Nedarim* 41a; see also *Ketuvot* 68a.

26. The issue at hand is essentially that of "clean" wealth. For more on the positive Jewish approach to wealth and its role in rectifying reality, see *Ma'ayan Ganim* on *Parshat Vayigash*.

Chapter 8

1. In our model, the decision stage (*hachlatat ha'da'at*) is characterized as the product of our choice being subjected to clarification and is associated with the *sefirah* of foundation, the last of the six forces of clarification. The Hebrew word for decision

(*hachlatah*) is based on the same root as the word for absolute (*muchlat*), thereby alluding to the absolutist character restored to one's choices once the process of clarity has been allowed to run its course.

2. Genesis 3:24; 4:1.

3. *Rambam Hilchot Ishut* 4:1.

This opinion is based upon the *braita* (*Kidushin* 9b) that states: "We only write marriage contracts in accordance with the knowledge of both of them." In the context of our discussion, we can interpret "the knowledge of both of them" as an allusion to the *da'at elyon* ("higher consciousness") of the groom and the *da'at tachton* ("lower consciousness") of his prospective bride.

4. *Midrash Bereishit Rabbah* 17:7. The Midrash reads as follows: "It is told that there was once a pious man married to a pious woman, who were unable to have children. They declared, 'Behold we are of no use to the Holy One.' So they got up and divorced one another. He went and married an evil woman, who made him wicked as well. She went and married an evil man, but made him righteous. Hence we see that everything depends upon the woman." See also *Shechinah Beineihem*, p. 55, footnote 34.

5. As reflected in the verse: "I have put before you life and death, the blessing and the curse—choose life...." (Deuteronomy 30:19).

6. *Berachot* 8a.

7. Proverbs 18:22.

8. Ecclesiastes 7:26. There is another verse that highlights the antagonism between the wicked woman and the path of life: "Instructive rebukes are the path of life to preserve you from the wicked woman" (Proverbs 6:24).

9. Ecclesiastes 9:9.

10. The most significant example of this usage appears in the Torah's account of the binding of Isaac. Twice, in relating that event, the Torah employs the root of the verb "to see" (*ra'ah*) to connote an act of choosing (see Genesis 22:8, 14 and Rashi's commentary there).

11. There is a similar text appearing earlier that states: "See, I place before you today a blessing and a curse; the blessing if you heed the commandments of God... and the curse if you do not heed the commandments of God...." (Deuteronomy 11:26-28). Although there is no explicit mention of choice, it is certainly implicit in the way the "blessing" and the "curse" are presented— terms that themselves reappear in Deuteronomy 30:19 exhorting one to "choose life."

12. See *Kidushin* 30b where the verse "see life with the woman whom you love" (Ecclesiastes 9:9) is brought in context of a man's obligation to acquire a vocation (especially as a requirement for getting married). The Talmud there dwells on the words "see life," meaning "be able to make a living." But, as pointed out by some medieval commentaries, "making a living" in this verse seems to depend on "with the woman whom you love." In other words, a couple's livelihood also depends on the woman and her approach to life.

13. As noted earlier, the light-illuminating-oneself is identified with higher consciousness, and the light-illuminating-another is identified with lower consciousness. The "self-reflection" of higher consciousness produces those deep-rooted identifications that serve as the basis for the direct light that is projected onto outer reality. By emotionally investing ourselves in illuminating another, we absorb the energy emitted by that person's reality (reflected light) and channel it back into our own consciousness. It is by means of this interaction between the direct light and the reflected light that the signals of inner and outer experience may resolve themselves.

14. See "Clarification by Direct and Reflected Light" (p. 189).

15. Proverbs 12:4.

Chapter 9

1. Objectivity of consciousness (*nekiyut hada'at*) refers to clear-headedness and is derived from the reference in the Talmud (*Sanhedrin* 23a) to the "clear-headed" Jerusalemites who would refuse to sign as witnesses to a contract, participate in tribunals, or partake in feasts unless they could personally vouch for the character of those who were to join them in these activities. These customs demonstrate how the reluctance to be drawn into a premature identification with others might translate into direct practice. The last of these customs—the refusal to partake in feasts with strangers—best expresses the fear of negative influence that opposes one's desire to cultivate friendships through drink and merriment (as stated in *Sanhedrin* 103b: "Great is imbibing for it brings people together").

2. *Sotah* 47a. *Zohar* III:177b.

3. According to Chassidic thought (see the Hebrew volume *Sod Hashem Liye'reiav* pp. 188ff.), the initial altruism (*ratzon leheitiv*) that inspired God to create the world had to be complimented by a corresponding drive referred to as the Divine thought of "I shall rule" (*ana emloch*). The effect of this yearning for sovereignty was to guarantee that the need for order and discipline in creation would restrain God's innate desire to bestow goodness indiscriminately. The destructive consequences of unrestrained Divine benevolence are reflected in the Talmudic reference to the

first 2000 years of creation as "the millennia of chaos [*tohu*]" (*Senhedrin* 97a; *Avoda Zarah* 9a).

Underlying this reference is the teaching of the sages (*Pesachim* 118a) that during this period of creation's "infancy" (that lasted twenty-six generations) God sustained the world primarily through benevolence—flooding reality with a Divine light that the world was not yet mature enough to appreciate. This situation led to a state of chaos whereby man, even as he beheld the benevolence of his Creator, rose in rebellion against Him. This rebellion is personified by King Nimrod (Genesis 10:8), whose name comes from the Hebrew word meaning "to rebel," and who was the leader of the generation known as "the generation of divisiveness," the generation that built the Tower of Babel (*Chulin* 89a).

4. Proverbs 27:19.

5. The identification of "grace" with humility is alluded to by these two similar verses from Proverbs: "the lowly of spirit shall sustain honor" (29:23), and "a woman of grace shall sustain honor" (11:16).

6. Isaiah 29:19. For a more extensive treatment of the basic psychology and beliefs underlying different behavioral responses see the article *"Perek Be'avodat Hashem"* in *Lev Lada'at*.

7. This phrase, which represents a variation on the Kabbalistic concept of reaching-and-not-reaching (*mati velo mati*), has its source in Rashi's interpretation of the word hovering (*yerachef*) in the verse: "as an eagle awaking its nest, hovering over its young ones" (Deuteronomy 32:11). The grammatical root of hovering, רחף, first appears in the second verse of the Torah: "and the spirit of God was hovering (*merachefet*) over the face of the waters" (Genesis 1:2), where its implication is also that of God's touching-and-not-touching creation.

8. It is appropriate here to mention that in the context of religious dating, during which Jewish law demands modesty (*tzniut*)

and restraint from physical contact, the framework for objectivity (*nekiyut hada'at*) is already built into the relationship. This leaves the couple free to focus on developing their affinity (*kiruv hada'at*) in a way that avoids the often narcissistic trap of physical interaction.

9. *Eiruvin* 100a.

10. The archetypal example of a Divine "pointing finger" is to be found in the Midrash where the child Moses is depicted as "choosing" between gold and embers. Inserting the glowing coals into his mouth, Moses became hard of speech, a Divinely ordained condition which in its essence prepared him for his role as the redeemer (see *Shemot Rabbah* 1:26).

11. Based on the verse "Jacob that redeemed Abraham" (Isaiah 29:22), the *Tanya* (chapter 32) explains that compassion (*rachamim*, the inner experience of the *sefirah* of beauty, identified with Jacob) "redeems" love (*ahavah*, the inner experience of the *sefirah* of loving-kindness, identified with Abraham). Thus, disillusioned or broken feelings of love may be restored or rehabilitated by arousing, through contemplation, sentiments of compassion for the other's soul.

12. Genesis 1:28.

13. Psalms 15:2. See also *Baba Batra* 88a for how this applies to one's relationships, business and otherwise, especially Rashi on the words "*Rav Safra.*"

14. Regarding the oath administered to each person before they are born and discussed in the opening chapter of the *Tanya*, it is explained in later writings of Chassidut that the nature of this oath is a form of empowerment from the person's higher spiritual source, known as *tikun ve'emet*, the seventh of the *tikunei dikna* (see also the discourse titled "*Chag Shavuot*" in *Sefer Hama'marim 5698*).

15. *Keter elyon ihu keter malchut.* Introduction (*Patach Eliyahu*) to *Tikunei Zohar.*

16. "A women 'speaks' with her husband" in *Berachot* 3a.

17. See footnote in the Lubavitcher Rebbe's *Likutei Sichot*, volume 8, p. 348 and locations cited there.

18. In *Hayom Yom* for 29th of Tishrei, the following story is told:

> One of the burghers of Mezhibezh had an argument with another burgher. When in shul with the Ba'al Shem Tov he was heard screaming that he would like to tear his opponent like a fish.
>
> The Ba'al Shem Tov told his disciples to join hands and stand in a circle with their eyes closed. The Ba'al Shem Tov placed his own holy hands on the shoulders of the two disciples to his left and right. All at once the disciples began to scream in terror, for they saw how the burgher indeed tore his opponent like a fish.
>
> This story clearly relates how actual results ensue from all the powers of the soul, whether in a physical garb or in a spiritual garb, which can only be experienced with higher, more refined faculties.

19. Rabbi Moshe ibn Ezra's *Shirat Yisrael* p. 156 (see Lubavitcher Rebbe's *Igrot Kodesh* volume 3, epistle 448).

20. *Megilah* 29a. The Lubavitcher Rebbe entreated time and again that we should all make our homes like a shul, and as a place where Torah and prayer and acts of charity are nurtured.

21. "God yearned to create his abode below" (*Midrash Tanchuma Nasso* 15).

Glossary

Note: all foreign terms are Hebrew unless otherwise indicated. Terms preceded by an asterisk have their own entries.

Abba (אַבָּא, "father" [Aramaic]): the *partzuf* of *chochmah.

Adam Kadmon (אָדָם קַדְמוֹן, "primordial man"): the first *world.

Arich Anpin (אֲרִיךְ אַנְפִּין, "the long face" or "the infinitely patient one"): the external *partzuf* of *keter (the inner dimension is *Atik Yomin). In psychological terms, it is synonymous with will. It possesses its own *keter* (the *gulgalta*), and its own *chochmah (*mocha stima'ah).

Asiyah (עֲשִׂיָּה, "action"): the lowest of the four *worlds.

Atbash: (אַתְבַּ"שׁ): the simple reflective transformation. The first letter of the alphabet is paired with the last, the second with the second-to-last, and so on. Letters in each pair may then be interchanged.

כ	י	ט	ח	ז	ו	ה	ד	ג	ב	א
ל	מ	נ	ס	ע	פ	צ	ק	ר	שׁ	ת

Atik: short for *Atik Yomin.

Atik Yomin (עַתִּיק יוֹמִין, the ancient of days" [Aramaic]): the inner *partzuf* of *keter.

Atika Kadisha (עַתִּיקָא קַדִּישָׁא, "the holy ancient One" [Aramaic]): in some contexts, this term is a synonym for *Atik Yomin; in others, for *keter in general.

Av (אָב, "father"): the fifth month of the Jewish calendar.

Ba'al Shem Tov (בַּעַל שֵׁם טוֹב, "Master of the Good Name [of God]"): Title of Rabbi Yisrael ben Eliezer (1698-1760), founder of the Chassidic movement (see *Chassidut*).

Ba'al Teshuvah (בַּעַל תְּשׁוּבָה, "one who returns"): one who returns to the ways of Judaism and adherence to Jewish law after a period of estrangement. Often used in contrast to a **tzadik*, who has not undergone such a period. The *ba'al teshuvah* strives continually to ascend, return and become subsumed within God's essence; the *tzadik* strives primarily to serve God by doing good deeds and thus drawing His light into the world. Ideally these two paths are meant to be inter-included, i.e. that every Jew should embody both the service of the *ba'al teshuvah* and that of the *tzadik*, as well. See also *teshuvah*.

Binah (בִּינָה, "understanding"): the third of the ten **sefirot*.

Birur (בֵּרוּר, "clarification," "choosing," or "refinement"): a type of **tikun* in which one must work to separate good from evil in any given entity, and then reject the evil and accept the good. This may be done actively or in one's consciousness. See also **yichud*.

Bitachon (בִּטָּחוֹן, "confidence"): 1. the feeling of confidence in one's God-given power to take initiative and succeed in one's mission in life. See **emunah*. 2. The inner experience of the **sefirah* of **netzach*. 3. ("trust"): the feeling that God will orchestrate events in accord with the greatest revealed good. This passive *bitachon* is associated with the *sefirah* of **hod*.

Bitul (בִּטּוּל, "annihilation"): any of a number of states of selflessness or self-abnegation. The inner experience of the **sefirah* of **chochmah*.

Brit (בְּרִית, "covenant") or ***brit milah*** (בְּרִית מִילָה, "covenant of circumcision"): 1. the covenant or eternal bond God made with Abraham and the Jewish people, indicated by the circumcision of the male reproductive organ, usually on the eighth day after birth. 2. The ceremony at which this commandment is performed. 3. Euphemism for the male reproductive organ itself.

Chabad (חַבַּ"ד) acronym for **chochmah*, **binah*, **da'at* (חָכְמָה בִּינָה דַּעַת, "wisdom, understanding, knowledge"): 1. the first triad of **sefirot*, which constitute the intellect (see also *Chagat, Nehi*). 2. the branch of **Chassidut* founded by Rabbi Shneur Zalman of Liadi (1745-1812), emphasizing the role of the intellect and meditation in the service of God.

Chagat (חַגַ"ת) acronym for **chesed*, **gevurah*, **tiferet* (חֶסֶד גְּבוּרָה תִּפְאֶרֶת, "loving-kindness, strength, and beauty"): the second triad of **sefirot*, which together constitute the primary emotions (see also *Chabad, Nehi*).

Chasadim: plural of **chesed* (second sense).

Chassidut (חַסִידוּת, "piety" or "loving-kindness"): 1. An attribute or way of life that goes beyond the letter of the law. 2. The movement within Judaism founded by Rabbi Yisrael Ba'al Shem Tov (1648-1760), the purpose of which is to awaken the Jewish people to its own inner self through the inner dimension of the Torah and thus to prepare the way for the advent of **Mashiach*. 3. The oral and written teachings of this movement.

Chayah (חַיָּה, "living one"): the second highest of the five levels of the **soul*.

Chesed (חֶסֶד, "loving-kindness"; pl. חֲסָדִים *chasadim*): 1. the fourth of the ten **sefirot*. 2. a manifestation of this attribute, specifically in **da'at*.

Chochmah (חָכְמָה, "wisdom" or "insight"): the second of the ten **sefirot*.

Da'at (דַּעַת, "knowledge"): 1. the unifying force within the ten **sefirot*. 2. the third **sefirah* of the intellect, counted as one of the ten *sefirot* when **keter* is not.

Din (דִּין, "judgment; pl. דִּינִים, *dinim*): 1. a synonym for **gevurah*. 2. a manifestation of this attribute. 3. a synonym for **kal vechomer*.

Emunah (אֱמוּנָה, "faith" or "belief"): 1. the belief that no matter what God does, it is all ultimately for the greatest good, even if it does not appear so to us presently; see **bitachon*. 2. the inner experience associated with **Reisha d'lo Ityada*.

Gematria (גִּימַטְרִיָּא, "numerology" [Aramaic]): the technique of comparing Hebrew words and phrases based on their numerical values.

Gevurah (גְּבוּרָה, "strength" or "might"; pl. גְּבוּרוֹת, *gevurot*): 1. the fifth of the ten *sefirot*. 2. a manifestation of this attribute, specifically in *da'at*.

Gevurot: plural of *gevurah* (second sense).

Gulgalta (גֻּלְגַּלְתָּא, "the skull" [Aramaic]): the *keter* of *Arich Anpin*. In psychological terms, the interface between pleasure and will, which serves as the origin of the super-conscious will.

Halachah (הֲלָכָה, "way" or "walking): 1. the entire corpus of Jewish law. 2. a specific Jewish law.

Havayah (יְהוּ-ה): also known as the Tetragrammaton ("four-letter Name"). Due to its great sanctity, this Name may only be pronounced in the Holy Temple, and its correct pronunciation is not known today. When one is reciting a complete Scriptural verse or liturgy, it is read as if it were the Name *Adni*; otherwise one says *Hashem* (הַשֵּׁם, "the Name") or *Havayah* (הֲוָיָה a permutation of the four letters of this Name).

Havayah is the most sacred of God's Names. Although no name can fully express God's essence, the Name *Havayah* in certain contexts *refers* to God's essence. In these cases it is called "the higher Name *Havayah*" and is termed "the essential Name" (שֵׁם הָעֶצֶם), "the unique Name" (שֵׁם הַמְיֻחָד), and "the explicit Name" (שֵׁם הַמְפֹרָשׁ).

Otherwise, the Name *Havayah* refers to God as He manifests Himself through creation. In these cases it is called "the lower Name *Havayah*," and its four letters are seen to depict in their form the creative process and allude to the worlds, ten *sefirot*, etc., as follows:

	creation	worlds	sefirot
י upper tip of *yud*	will to create	*Adam Kadmon*	*keter*
י *yud*	contraction	*Atzilut*	*chochmah*
ה *hei*	expansion	*Beriah*	*binah*
ו *vav*	extension	*Yetzirah*	the six *midot*
ה *hei*	expansion	*Asiyah*	*malchut*

The lower Name *Havayah* appears on several levels. It is first manifest as the light within all the *sefirot*. It thus possesses on this level ten iterations, which are indicated as ten vocalizations—each using one of the ten vowels. (These are only meditative "vocalizations," since it is forbidden to pronounce the Name *Havayah* with any vocalization, as we have said.) For example, when each of its four letters is vocalized with a *kamatz*, it signifies the light within the *sefirah* of *keter*; when they are each vocalized with a *patach*, it signifies the light within the *sefirah* of *chochmah*. The other Names of God (including the subsequent manifestations of the Name *Havayah*) refer to the vessels of the *sefirot*. In the world of *Atzilut*, where these Names are principally manifest, both the vessels and the lights of the *sefirot* are manifestations of Divinity.

The second manifestation of the lower Name *Havayah* is as the vessel of the *sefirah* of *chochmah*. (This is alluded to in the verse, "*Havayah* in *chochmah* founded the earth" [*Proverbs* 3:19].)

Its third manifestation is as the vessel of the *sefirah* of *binah*. This manifestation is indicated by the consonants of the Name vocalized with the vowels of (and read as) the Name *Elokim* (for example, *Deuteronomy* 3:24, etc.).

The most basic manifestation of the lower Name *Havayah* is in the *sefirah* of *tiferet*, whose inner experience is mercy. The Name

Havayah in general is associated with "the principle of mercy," since mercy is the most basic emotion through which God relates to His creation. In this, its most common sense, it is vocalized with the vowels of (and read as) the Name *Adnut*.

Hod (הוֹד, "splendor," "thanksgiving," "acknowledgment"): the eighth of the ten *sefirot*.

Ima (אָמָּא, "mother" [Aramaic]): the *partzuf* of *binah*.

Kabbalah (קַבָּלָה, "receiving" or "tradition"): the esoteric dimension of the Torah.

Kav (קַו, "line"): the ray of light beamed into the vacated space created in consequence of the *tzimtzum*.

Keter (כֶּתֶר, "crown"): the first of the ten *sefirot*.

Lights: see *Sefirah*.

Lubavitch (לְיוּבַּאוִויטְשׁ, "City of Love" [Russian]): the town that served as the center of the *Chabad* movement from 1812 to 1915; the movement became known also after the name of this town.

Malchut (מַלְכוּת, "kingdom"): the last of the ten *sefirot*.

Mashiach (מָשִׁיחַ, "anointed one," "messiah"): the prophesied descendant of King David who will reinstate the Torah-ordained monarchy (which he will head), rebuild the Holy *Temple, and gather the exiled Jewish people to their homeland. This series of events (collectively called "the Redemption") will usher in an era of eternal, universal peace and true knowledge of God, called "the messianic era." There is also a prophesied messianic figure called *Mashiach ben* Joseph, who will rectify certain spiritual aspects of reality in preparation for the advent of *Mashiach ben* David.

Mazal (מַזָּל, pl. מַזָּלוֹת, *mazalot*): 1. a spiritual conduit of Divine beneficence (from the root נזל, "to flow"). 2. specifically, the thirteen tufts of the "beard" of *Arich Anpin*. 3. a physical embodiment of such a spiritual conduit, such as a star, planet, constellation, etc. 4. specifically, the twelve constellations of the zodiac. 5. According to our sages, the Jewish people are not under the influence of the *mazalot* (Shabbat 156a). The Ba'al Shem Tov teaches that the Divine "nothingness" itself is the true *mazal* of the Jewish people.

Midah (מִדָּה, "measure" or "attribute," pl. מִדּוֹת, *midot*): 1. an attribute of God. 2. specifically, one of the *sefirot from *chesed to *malchut, in contrast to the higher *sefirot* of the intellect. 3. one of the thirteen attributes of mercy, which are part of the revelation of *keter.

Midot: plural of *midah.

Midrash (מִדְרָשׁ, "seeking"; pl. מִדְרָשִׁים, *Midrashim*): the second major body of the oral Torah (after the *Talmud), consisting of halachic or homiletic material couched as linguistic analyses of the Biblical text. An individual work of midrashic material is also called a *Midrash*, as is a specific analysis in midrashic style.

The *Midrash* is a corpus of many works written over the span of several centuries (roughly the second to the eighth CE), mostly in the Holy Land. The chief collection of homiletic midrashic material is the *Rabbah* ("great") series, covering the five books of Moses and the five scrolls. Other important collections are *Midrash Tanchuma*, *Midrash Tehilim*, *Pesikta d'Rav Kahana*, *Pirkei d'Rabbi Eliezer* and *Tana d'vei Eliahu*. Several later collections contain material that has reached us in its original form. These include *Midrash HaGadol* and *Yalkut Shimoni*. There are many smaller, minor *Midrashim*, as well; some of these are to be found in the collection *Otzar HaMidrashim*. Halachic *Midrashim* include the *Mechilta*, the *Sifra* and the *Sifrei*.

Mitzvah (מִצְוָה, "commandment"; pl. מִצְוֹת, *mitzvot*): one of the six hundred thirteen commandments given by God to the Jewish people, or seven commandments given by God to the nations of the world, at Mt. Sinai. 2. one of the seven commandments instituted by the sages. 3. idiomatically, any good deed.

Mitzvot: plural of *mitzvah.

Mocha Stima'ah (מוֹחָא סְתִימָאָה, "the hidden brain" [Aramaic]): the *chochmah of *Arich Anpin. In psychological terms, the power to generate new insight (כֹּחַ הַמַּשְׂכִּיל).

Mochin d'Abba (מוֹחִין דְּאַבָּא, "brains of *Abba" [Aramaic]): a state of consciousness, mentality, or cognitive life force in which one experiences *chochmah, or insight.

Mochin d'Ima (מוֹחִין דְּאִמָּא, "brains of *Ima" [Aramaic]): a state of consciousness or mentality, or cognitive life force in which one experiences *binah, or understanding or rationality.

Nefesh (נֶפֶשׁ, "creature," "soul"): 1. the soul in general. 2. the lowest of the five levels of the *soul.

Nehi (נְהִ"י) acronym for *netzach, *hod, *yesod (נֵצַח הוֹד יְסוֹד, "victory, splendor, foundation": the third triad of *sefirot, which together constitute the attributes of behavior (see *Chabad, Chagat*).

Neshamah (נְשָׁמָה, "soul"): 1. the soul in general. 2. the third of the five levels of the *soul.

Netzach (נֵצַח, "victory," "eternity"): the seventh of the ten *sefirot.

Notrikon (נוֹטָרִיקוֹן, "acronym"): a hermeneutic method in which the letters of a word are interpreted as the initials or main consonantal letters of a different word or phrase.

Nukvei d'Z'eir Anpin (נוּקְבֵיהּ דִּזְעֵיר אַנְפִּין [Aramaic]): the *partzuf of *malchut.

Partzuf (פַּרְצוּף, "profile," "persona"; pl. פַּרְצוּפִים, *partzufim*): the third and final stage in the development of a *sefirah, in which it metamorphoses from a tenfold articulation of sub-*sefirot* into a human-like figure possessing the full set of intellectual and emotional powers. As such, it may thus interact with the other *partzufim* (which could not occur before this transformation. This stage of development constitutes the transition from *Tohu to *Tikun (or from *Nekudim* to *Berudim*, see under Worlds).

Within any particular *partzuf*, the *sefirot* are arranged along three axes, right, left and middle, as follows:

left axis	center axis	right axis
	keter	
binah		*chochmah*
	da'at	
gevurah		*chesed*
	tiferet	
hod		*netzach*
	yesod	
	malchut	

In this arrangement, there are three triads of related *sefirot*: *chochmah-binah-da'at* (the intellect), *chesed-gevurah-tiferet* (the primary emotions) and *netzach-hod-yesod* (the behavioral attributes).

The *sefirot* develop into a primary and a secondary array of *partzufim*, as follows:

sefirah	primary *partzufim*		secondary *partzufim*	
keter	עַתִּיק יוֹמִין *Atik Yomin*	"The Ancient of Days"	עַתִּיק יוֹמִין *Atik Yomin*	[The male dimension of] "the Ancient of Days"
			נוּקְבֵיהּ דְּעַתִּיק יוֹמִין *Nukvei d'Atik Yomin*	[The female dimension of] "the Ancient of Days"
	אֲרִיךְ אַנְפִּין *Arich Anpin*	"The Long Face"	אֲרִיךְ אַנְפִּין *Arich Anpin*	[The male dimension of] "the Long Face"
			נוּקְבֵיהּ דְּאֲרִיךְ אַנְפִּין *Nukvei d'Arich Anpin*	[The female dimension of] "the Long Face"
chochmah	אַבָּא *Abba*	"Father"	אַבָּא עִילָאָה *Abba Ila'ah*	"Supernal Father"
			אִמָּא עִילָאָה *Ima Ila'ah*	"Supernal Mother"
binah	אִמָּא *Ima*	"Mother"	יִשְׂרָאֵל סַבָּא *Yisrael Saba*	"Israel the Elder"
			תְּבוּנָה *Tevunah*	"Understanding"
the midot	זְעֵיר אַנְפִּין *Z'eir Anpin*	"The Small Face"	יִשְׂרָאֵל *Yisrael*	"Israel"
			לֵאָה *Leah*	"Leah"
malchut	נוּקְבֵיהּ דִּזְעֵיר אַנְפִּין *Nukvei d'Z'eir Anpin*	"The Female of Z'eir Anpin"	יַעֲקֹב *Yaakov*	"Jacob"
			רָחֵל *Rachel*	"Rachel"

Both of the secondary, male and female *partzufim* of *Atik Yomin* and *Arich Anpin* exist within the same figure. There are thus actually only ten distinct secondary *partzufim*.

Rachamim (רַחֲמִים, "mercy"): the inner experience of the *sefirah* of *tiferet*.

Reisha d'Arich (רֵישָׁא דַּאֲרִיךְ, "the head of *Arich [Anpin]*" [Aramaic]): the lowest of the three heads of the *keter*, synonymous with the **partzuf* of *Arich Anpin*. In psychological terms, super-conscious will.

Reisha d'Ayin (רֵישָׁא דְּאַיִן, "the head of nothingness" [Aramaic]): the middle of the three heads of the **keter*, related to the emotions of the **partzuf* of **Atik Yomin*. In psychological terms, super-conscious pleasure.

Reisha d'Lo Ityada (רֵישָׁא דְּלֹא אִתְיָדַע, "the unknowable head" [Aramaic]): the highest of the three heads of the **keter*, related to the keter and intellect of the **partzuf* of **Atik Yomin*. In psychological terms, super-conscious belief in God.

Rebbe (רַבִּי, "my teacher"): 1. a term used to describe or address a teacher of Torah. 2. leader of a branch · of the Chassidic movement.

Reshimu (רְשִׁימוּ, "residue," "impression"): the residual impression of the infinite Divine light that God withdrew from the vacated space resulting from the **tzimtzum*.

Rosh Chodesh (ראֹשׁ חדֶֹשׁ, "new month"): the first day of a Jewish month, a day of celebration.

Rosh HaShanah (ראֹשׁ הַשָּׁנָה, "beginning of the year"): the Jewish New Year, commemorating the creation of man on the sixth day of creation, a day of universal judgment.

Ruach (רוּחַ, "spirit"): a level of the **soul.

Sabbath: see *Shabbat*.

Sages: see *Torah*.

Sefirah (סְפִירָה, pl. סְפִירוֹת, *sefirot*): a channel of Divine energy or life force. It is via the *sefirot* that God interacts with creation; they may thus be considered His "attributes."

There are altogether eleven *sefirot* spoken of in Kabbalistic literature. Inasmuch as two of them (*keter* and *da'at*) are two dimensions of a single force, the tradition generally speaks of only ten *sefirot*. Each *sefirah* also possesses an inner experience, as discussed in **Chassidut*. The order of the *sefirot* is depicted in the following chart:

name			inner experience	
keter	כֶּתֶר	"crown"	אֱמוּנָה תַּעֲנוּג רָצוֹן	1. "faith" 2. "pleasure" 3. "will"
chochmah	חָכְמָה	"wisdom," "insight"	בִּטּוּל	"selflessness"
binah	בִּינָה	"understanding"	שִׂמְחָה	"joy"
da'at	דַּעַת	"knowledge"	יִחוּד	"union"
chesed	חֶסֶד	"loving- kindness"	אַהֲבָה	"love"
gevurah	גְּבוּרָה	"strength," "might"	יִרְאָה	"fear"
tiferet	תִּפְאֶרֶת	"beauty"	רַחֲמִים	"mercy"
netzach	נֶצַח	"victory," "eternity"	בִּטָּחוֹן	"confidence"
hod	הוֹד	"splendor," "thanksgiving"	תְּמִימוּת	"sincerity," "earnestness"
yesod	יְסוֹד	"foundation"	אֱמֶת	"truth"
malchut	מַלְכוּת	"kingdom"	שִׁפְלוּת	"humility"

Originally emanated as simple point-like forces, the *sefirot* at a certain stage develop into full spectrums of ten sub-*sefirot*. Subsequent to this, they metamorphose into *partzufim.

Sefirot are composed of "lights" and "vessels." The light of any *sefirah* is the Divine flow within it; the vessel is the identity that flow takes in order to relate to or create some aspect of the world in a specific way. Inasmuch as all reality is created by means of the *sefirot*, they constitute the conceptual paradigm for understanding all reality.

Sefirot: plural of *sefirah.

Shabbat (שַׁבָּת, "Sabbath"): the day of rest beginning sunset on Friday and ending at nightfall on Saturday.

Shacharit (שַׁחֲרִית, "morning"): the morning prayer service.

Shechinah (שְׁכִינָה, "indwelling"): the immanent Divine Presence that inheres within the universe, corresponding to the **sefirah* of **malchut*, the "feminine" aspect of Divinity.

Shema (שְׁמַע, "hear): a compilation of three Biblical passages (*Deuteronomy* 6:4-9, 11:13-21, *Numbers* 15:37-41) beginning with this word, or sometimes, the first verse alone. The first verse is the fundamental profession of monotheism, "Hear O Israel, *God* is our God, *God* is one." We are commanded to recite the *Shema* twice daily, and it has been incorporated into the morning and evening services as well as the prayer said upon retiring at night. When reciting the first sentence, we are intended to consider ourselves ready to give up our lives rather than deny the oneness of God.

Shemini Atzeret (שְׁמִינִי עֲצֶרֶת, "the eighth-day gathering"): the **yom tov* immediately following **Sukot*, marking the end of the high-holiday season.

Soul: the animating life or consciousness within man (or any other creature, see *Sha'ar HaYichud VehaEmunah*, ch. 1). The Jew possesses an additional "Divine soul" which is focused on God's concerns in creation.

The essence of the soul possesses five manifestations ("names"), as follows:

name			experience
yechidah	יְחִידָה	"unique one"	unity with God
chayah	חַיָּה	"living being"	awareness of God creating the world continuously
neshamah	נְשָׁמָה	"breath"	vitality of intelligence
ruach	רוּחַ	"spirit"	vitality of emotion
nefesh	נֶפֶשׁ	"creature"	physical vitality

Taharah (טָהֳרָה, ritual "purity"): the spiritual state in which one purified himself from a specific degree of **tumah* (or from *tumah* altogether), and is thus allowed to enter areas or touch, be touched by, or consume things or food he otherwise may not. In general, the process of attaining *taharah* involves some type of reaffirmation of life, such as immersion in a **mikveh*. The spiritual correlate to *taharah* is optimistic elation or joy in the service of God. See *tumah*.

Talmud: (תַּלְמוּד, "learning"): the written version of the greater part of the Oral *Torah, comprising mostly legal but also much homiletic and even some explicitly mystical material.

The *Talmud* comprises the *Mishnah* (מִשְׁנָה, "repetition") and the *Gemara* (גְּמָרָא, "completion"). The *Mishnah* is the basic compendium of the laws (each known as a *mishnah*) comprising the Oral Torah, redacted by Rabbi Yehudah the Prince in the second century CE. The *Mishnah* was elaborated upon over the next few centuries in the academies of the Holy Land and Babylonia; this material is the *Gemara*.

There are thus two *Talmuds*: the one composed in the Holy Land, known as the *Talmud Yerushalmi* ("The Jerusalem *Talmud*"), completed in the third century, and the one composed in Babylonia, known as the *Talmud Bavli* ("The Babylonian *Talmud*), completed in the sixth century.

The *Mishnah*—and *ipso facto* the *Talmud*—is divided into tractates. References to the *Mishnah* are simply the name of the tractate followed by the number of the chapter and individual *mishnah*.

The Jerusalem Talmud was first printed in Venice, 1523-24. Although subsequent editions have generally followed the same pagination as this edition, it is nonetheless cited by chapter and *halachah* (i.e., individual *mishnah*) number, as is the *Mishnah*. References to it are therefore prefaced by "*Y.*," to distinguish them from references to the *Mishnah* itself. The Babylonian Talmud was first printed in its entirety in Venice, 1520-23, and subsequent editions have followed the same pagination as this edition. References to the tractates of the *Talmud Bavli* are simply by tractate name followed by leaf and page ("a" or "b").

Temimut (תְּמִימוּת, "sincerity"): 1. earnestness and sincerity, either in one's conduct with his fellow man or in his connection to God. 2. The inner experience of *hod.

Temple (or "Holy Temple"; Hebrew: בֵּית הַמִּקְדָּשׁ, "house of the sanctuary"): The central sanctuary in Jerusalem which serves as the physical abode of the indwelling of God's Presence on earth and as the venue for the sacrificial service. The Temple is the focal point of one's spiritual consciousness. The first Temple was built by King Solomon (833 BCE) and destroyed by the Babylonians (423 BCE); the second Temple was built by Zerubabel (synonymous, according to some opinions, with Nehemiah, 353 BCE), remodeled by Herod and destroyed by the Romans (68 CE); the third, eternal Temple will be built by *Mashiach*.

Teshuvah (תְּשׁוּבָה, "return"): the return of the individual (or community), after a period of estrangement, to a state of oneness with and commitment to God and His Torah. See *Ba'al Teshuvah*.

Tevunah (תְּבוּנָה, "comprehension"): the lower of the two secondary *partzufim* which develop from the *partzuf* of *Ima*, the higher one being *Ima Ila'ah* (אִמָּא עִילָאָה).

Tiferet (תִּפְאֶרֶת, "beauty"): the sixth of the ten *sefirot*.

Tikun (תִּקּוּן, "rectification," pl. תִּקּוּנִים, *tikunim*): 1. a state of perfection and order. 2. "The world of *Tikun*" is the *world that first manifests this state, which is synonymous with the world of *Atzilut* (and *Berudim*, see Worlds). 3. the spiritual process of liberating the fragments of Divine light trapped within the material realm, unconscious of God's presence, thereby restoring the world to its initially intended state of perfection. This is accomplished through the performance of *mitzvot*. 4. a remedy prescribed against the effects of committing a specific sin.

Tikunim: plural of *tikun* (fourth sense).

Tohu (תֹהוּ, "chaos"): 1. the primordial, unrectified state of creation. 2. "The world of *Tohu*" is the *world which manifests this state, synonymous with the initial, premature form of the world of *Atzilut*. It itself develops in two stages: a stable form (*Akudim*) followed by an unstable form (*Nekudim*, see Worlds).

The world of *Tohu* is characterized by "great lights" entering premature "vessels," resulting in the (שְׁבִירַת הַכֵּלִים) "breaking of the vessels." See *Tikun*.

Torah (תּוֹרָה, "teaching"): God's will and wisdom as communicated to man. It pre-existed creation, and God used the Torah as His blueprint in creating the world.

God certainly communicated the teachings of the Torah in some form to Adam, who then transmitted them orally from generation to generation. However, God "officially" gave the Torah to mankind c. 1313 BCE (and during the ensuing 40 years) at Mt. Sinai through Moses. The Ten Commandments were pronounced in the presence of the entire Jewish people.

God gave the Torah in two parts: the Written Torah and the Oral Torah. The Written Torah originally consisted of the Five Books of Moses (the "Pentateuch"), the other books being added later (see Bible). The Oral Torah was communicated together with the Five Books of Moses as an explanation of the laws and lore included in it. This material was later written down by the sages of the Oral Torah in the form of the *Talmud*, the *Midrash*, and the *Zohar*. (All references to "our sages" in this book refer to the sages who transmitted the Oral Torah as recorded in these works.)

Tzadik (צַדִּיק, "righteous" person; pl. צַדִּיקִים, *tzadikim*): someone who has fully overcome the evil inclination of his animal soul (and converted its potential into good). See *beinoni, rasha*.

Tzadikim: plural of *tzadik*.

Tzimtzum (צִמְצוּם, "contraction"): the contraction and "removal" of God's infinite light in order to allow for creation of independent realities. The primordial *tzimtzum* produced the "vacated space" (חָלָל) devoid of direct awareness of God's presence. See *Kav* and *Reshimu*.

Vessels: see *sefirah*.

World (Hebrew: עוֹלָם): a spiritual level of creation, representing a rung on the continuum of consciousness or awareness of God. In general, there are four worlds: *Atzilut, *Beriah, *Yetzirah, and *Asiyah*. In particular, however, these four worlds originate from a fifth, higher world, *Adam Kadmon*. All ten *sefirot* and twelve *partzufim* are manifest in each world; however, since there is a one-to-one correspondence between the worlds and the *sefirot*, a particular *sefirah* dominates in each world.

The world of *Atzilut* is fundamentally different from the three subsequent worlds in that in it there is no awareness of self *per se*, while the three lower worlds are progressive stages in the development of self-awareness.

The worlds correspond to the Name *Havayah* and the *sefirot* as follows:

the Name *Havayah*	world	dominant sefirah	level of consciousness
י upper tip of *yud*	אָדָם קַדְמוֹן *Adam Kadmon* "Primordial Man"	*keter*	Divine will to create; plan of creation
י	אֲצִילוּת *Atzilut* "Emanation"	*chochmah*	solely of God; no self- awareness
ה	בְּרִיאָה *Beriah* "Creation"	*binah*	potential existence; formless substance
ו	יְצִירָה *Yetzirah* "Formation"	*midot*	general existence: archetypes, species
ה	עֲשִׂיָּה *Asiyah* "Action"	*malchut*	particular existence; individual creatures

In particular, the world of *Atzilut* develops out of *Adam Kadmon* in three stages (the names of which are taken from *Genesis* 30:10):

world		developmental stage	description	
עֲקֻדִּים *Akudim*	"bound," "striped"	ten lights in one vessel	stable chaos	תֹּהוּ *Tohu*
נְקֻדִּים *Nekudim*	"dotted," "spotted"	ten lights in ten vessels, unstable	unstable chaos, collapse	
בְּרֻדִּים *Berudim*	"patterned," "speckled"	ten lights in ten inter- included vessels; stable	stable, mature rectification	תִּקוּן *Tikun*

Whenever unqualified reference is made to the world of *Atzilut*, its final, mature stage is meant. It should be noted as well that our physical universe is *below* and "enclothes" the final two *sefirot* (*yesod* and *malchut*) of the spiritual world of *Asiyah* referred to above.

Yechidah (יְחִידָה, "single one"): the highest of the five levels of the *soul.

Yesod (יְסוֹד, "foundation"): the ninth of the ten *sefirot.

Yetzirah (יְצִירָה, "formation"): one of the four *worlds.

Yisrael Saba (יִשְׂרָאֵל סַבָּא, "Israel the Elder" [Aramaic]): the lower of the two secondary *partzufim* which develop from the *partzuf* of *Abba*, the higher being *Abba Ila'ah* (אַבָּא עִלָּאָה, "the higher Abba").

Yom Kippur (יוֹם כִּפּוּר, "Day of Atonement"): the holiest day of the Jewish year, marked by fasting and *teshuvah*, particularly through confession of sin.

Yom Tov (יוֹם טוֹב, "good day" or "holiday"): a festive holiday on which, with certain exceptions, weekday work is prohibited just as on *Shabbat.

Z'eir Anpin (זְעֵיר אַנְפִּין, "the small face" [Aramaic]): the *partzuf* of the *midot*, corresponding to the emotive faculties of the soul. In general, the concept of "finitude" or "finite power" is identified with Z'eir Anpin.

Zohar (זֹהַר, "Brilliance"): one of the basic texts of the oral *Torah and Kabbalah, recording the mystical teachings of Rabbi Shimon bar Yochai (2nd century). The Zoharic literature includes the *Zohar* proper, the *Tikunei Zohar*, and the *Zohar

Chadash. The *Zohar* was printed in 1558 in both Mantua and Cremona, but standard pagination follows the Mantua edition.

The Hebrew Alphabet, *Gematria* and "Filling"

The Hebrew Alphabet—known after its first two letters, *alef-beit* (אָלֶף-בֵּית)—comprises twenty-two letters, five of which possess a secondary form used at the end of a word. These letters are all consonants. Vowels are generally indicated as diacritical marks underneath, above, or after the letters; however, four of the twenty-two consonants indicate vowel-sounds as well, as will be explained.

	letter	name		sound
1	א	אָלֶף	*alef*	ʿ
2	ב	בֵּית	*beit*	b, v
3	ג	גִּימֶל	*gimel*	g
4	ד	דָּלֶת	*dalet*	d
5	ה	הֵא	*hei*	h
6	ו	וָו	*vav*	v
7	ז	זַיִן	*zayin*	z
8	ח	חֵית	*chet*	ch
9	ט	טֵית	*tet*	t
10	י	יוּד	*yud*	y
11	כ, ך	כָּף	*kaf*	k, ch

	letter	name		sound
12	ל	לָמֶד	*lamed*	l
13	מ, ם	מֵם	*mem*	m
14	נ, ן	נוּן	*nun*	n
15	ס	סָמֶךְ	*samech*	s
16	ע	עַיִן	*ayin*	ʿ
17	פ, ף	פֵּא	*pei*	p, f
18	צ, ץ	צָדִי	*tzadi*	tz
19	ק	קוּף	*kuf*	k
20	ר	רֵישׁ	*reish*	r
21	ש	שִׁין	*shin*	sh, s
22	ת	תָּו	*tav*	t

Gematria

Each letter possesses a numerical value. Thus, Hebrew words and phrases can be compared based on their numerical values. This technique is called *gematria* (גִּימַטְרִיָּא). There are several systems of *gematria*:

1. The system most generally used is the **absolute value** (מִסְפָּר הֶכְרֵחִי) or **normative value**. The letters are assigned numerical values in order, first the ones (1-9), then the tens (10-90), and then the hundreds (100-400). The final forms have the same values as their regular forms.

כ,ך	י	ט	ח	ז	ו	ה	ד	ג	ב	א
20	10	9	8	7	6	5	4	3	2	1

ת	ש	ר	ק	צ,ץ	פ,ף	ע	ס	נ,ן	מ,ם	ל
400	300	200	100	90	80	70	60	50	40	30

In a variation on this system, the five final forms are assigned the remaining hundreds, so that the last, twenty-seventh letter equals 900:

ס	נ	מ	ל	כ	י	ט	ח	ז	ו	ה	ד	ג	ב	א
60	50	40	30	20	10	9	8	7	6	5	4	3	2	1

ץ	ף	ן	ם	ך	ת	ש	ר	ק	צ	פ	ע
900	800	700	600	500	400	300	200	100	90	80	70

In this scheme, the thousands are indicated again from *alef* (which actual *means* "a thousand"), and thus the *alef-beit* becomes a complete cycle.

2. In the **ordinal value** system (מִסְפָּר סְדוּרִי), each of the twenty-two letters is given a value from one to twenty-two, in order.

3. In the **reduced value** system (מִסְפָּר קָטָן, "modulus 9" in mathematical terminology), each normative value of 10 and over is

reduced to a figure of one digit by ignoring the zeros of its normative value.

In both of these systems, just as in the case of the absolute value system, the final letters are sometimes considered to have the same numerical values as the regular forms and sometimes to possess their own numerical values.

ל	כ	י	ט	ח	ז	ו	ה	ד	ג	ב	א	letter
12	11	10	9	8	7	6	5	4	3	2	1	ordinal value
3	2	1	9	8	7	6	5	4	3	2	1	reduced value

ץ	ף	ן	ם	ך	ת	ש	ר	ק	צ	פ	ע	ס	נ	מ
27	26	25	24	23	22	21	20	19	18	17	16	15	14	13
9	8	7	6	5	4	3	2	1	9	8	7	6	5	4

4. In the **integral reduced value** system (מִסְפָּר קָטָן מִסְפָּרִי), the total value of a *word* (if more than 9) is reduced to one digit by repeatedly adding the integers of its value according to the normative, ordinal or reduced value systems (the same result will be obtained in each case). For example, the word for "peace," שלום = 376 in the normative system (300 ⊥ 30 ⊥ 6 ⊥ 40), 52 in the ordinal system (21 ⊥ 12 ⊥ 6 ⊥ 13), and 16 in the reduced system (3 ⊥ 3 ⊥ 6 ⊥ 4). The integral reduced value is obtained by adding either 3 ⊥ 7 ⊥ 6 = 16 and then adding again 1 ⊥ 6 to give 7; by adding 5 ⊥ 2 = 7; or by adding 1 ⊥ 6 = 7.

Reducing the full value of a letter or word to a smaller number is a process of *tzimtzum* ("contraction"), projecting the original range of meaning onto a lower level of consciousness. In the absolute system, the letters are assigned their full values. In the ordinal system, each letter still possesses a unique value, but the fundamental principle of consciousness reflected by the "base ten" ("decimal") system has disappeared. In the reduced system, the numbers are still calculated independently, but each letter no longer possesses a unique value. In the integral reduced system, the letters lose their independent identity altogether and disappear into the integral value of the word.

Thus, the four systems of *gematria* correspond to the four successive archetypal levels of consciousness of the four worlds, as follows:

In *Atzilut*, the *sefirot* are manifest in their fully developed and revealed form. Inasmuch as the *sefirot* are ten (*Sefer Yetzirah* 1:4: "ten and not nine, ten and not eleven"), the notion of assigning letters values based on the full decimal system is intrinsic to this world.

In *Beriah*, the lights of the *sefirot* (in which inhere the intrinsic principle of "ten and not nine...") disappear from view, leaving consciousness only of their vessels, in the form of a linear series of 22 letters. Awareness is thus no longer based on the decimal system. The letters are the building blocks of the words and constructs of thought.

In *Yetzirah*, the letters lose their unique values and become grouped into nine categories or species. Still, the letters retain their unique identities and thus there is awareness of creation being dependent on the Divine letters that make up the name of the creature.

In *Asiyah*, this awareness is also lost and the only force life seems dependent upon is the laws of nature, as represented by numbers *per se*.

absolute or normative value system	*Atzilut*
ordinal value system	*Beriah*
reduced value system	*Yetzirah*
integral reduced value system	*Asiyah*

There are also more complex systems of *gematria*. An example of these is the progressive system (מִסְפָּר קָדְמִי), in which the value of each letter is equal to the sum of the values of all the letters up to and including itself in the normative system. For example, the word for "water" (מים) = $(1 + 2 + 3 + 4 + 5 + 6 + 7 + 8 + 9 + 10 + 20 + 30 + 40) + (1 + 2 + 3 + 4 + 5 + 6 + 7 + 8 + 9 + 10) + (1 + 2 + 3 + 4 + 5 + 6 + 7 + 8 + 9 + 10 + 20 + 30 + 40) = 145 + 55 + 145 = 345$. This is the same as the value of the word for "Moses" (משה) in normative *gematria*. "And she called him 'Moses,' as she said: 'for I drew him out of the water'" (Exodus 2:10).

"Filling"

The "filling"—or, in Hebrew, *milui* (מִלּוּי)—of a word is obtained by spelling out the letters used to spell its name. The additional letters used to spell out the letters of the original word are considered to be "pregnant" within them. Once spelled out, the numerical value can then be calculated of the entire *milui*.

For example, the *milui* of the word for "grace," חן, is נון חית, which adds up to 524.

The names (*milui*) of some letters have variant spellings. The system of spellings given above is considered the simplest system, although it not necessarily the most frequently applied in Kabbalah. The most common variants are for the letters *hei* (הא, הה, הי), *vav* (וו, ואו, ויו), *pei* (פי, פה, פא), *tav* (תיו, תאו, תו), and *tzadi* (צדיק, צדי).

Indexes

Proper Names Index

Sources Index

Bible

Genesis

Subject Index